GLENCOE

PERSONAL FINANCE

Student Activity Workbook

McGraw Hill Glencoe

New York, New York Columbus, Ohio Chicago, Illinois Peoria, Illinois Woodland Hills, California

Glencoe

The McGraw-Hill Companies

Send all inquiries to:

Glencoe/McGraw-Hill
21600 Oxnard Street, Suite 500
Woodland Hills, CA 91367

ISBN 0-07-869289-X (Student Edition)
ISBN 0-07-869291-1 (Teacher Annotated Edition)

Printed in the United States of America.

1 2 3 4 5 6 7 8 9 024 08 07 06 05 04

TABLE OF CONTENTS

Unit 3 Investing Your Financial Resources

Unit 4 Protecting Your Finances

Student Class Instructor

Date Assigned Date Completed

CHAPTER 1 Personal Financial Planning

Reviewing Key Terms: Complete the Sentence

DIRECTIONS: *Using terms from the following list, complete the sentences below. Write the letter of the term you have chosen in the space provided.*

A. interest	F. opportunity cost
B. future value	G. personal financial planning
C. economics	H. present value
D. inflation	I. liquidity
E. Federal Reserve System	J. values

1. The price that is paid for the use of another's money is called ______.

2. The study of the decisions that go into making, distributing, and using goods and services is called ______.

3. ______ is the amount that your original deposit will be worth in the future, based on a specific interest rate over a specific period of time.

4. The central banking organization of the United States is known as the ______.

5. A possibility that you give up when you make one choice instead of another is commonly referred to as a(n) ______.

6. The ability to easily convert your financial resources to cash without a loss in value is called ______.

7. ______ is spending, saving, and investing your money so you can have the lifestyle you want as well as financial security.

8. ______ are the beliefs and principles you consider important, correct, and desirable.

9. ______ is the general rise in the level of prices for goods and services over time.

10. ______ is the amount of money you would need to deposit now to earn a desired amount in the future.

Student Class Instructor

Date Assigned Date Completed

CHAPTER 1 Personal Financial Planning

Understanding Key Concepts

DIRECTIONS: *On a separate sheet of paper, answer the questions below.*

1. Name two advantages of having a personal financial plan.
2. What role do values play in creating a personal financial plan? Provide two examples of how different values might lead to different financial goals.
3. With which type of investment would the liquidity risk be highest: a baseball card collection, a savings account, money hidden in a dresser drawer? Explain your answer.
4. After Alison graduates from high school and college, she's planning to go to medical school. She also wants to retire early so that she will have time to travel. Ty has just graduated from high school and wants to see the world. He has decided to postpone his education and career plans because he wants to travel as much as he can before he's 30. List one short-term goal, one intermediate goal, and one long-term goal that you might expect Alison to have. Do the same for Ty.
5. Categorize the following goods as consumable, durable, or intangible: a) tickets to a concert, b) leisure time, c) microwave oven, d) college education, e) gasoline for your car.
6. How might the popularity of a certain brand of clothing affect its price?
7. If the price of renting a video increases yearly based on the rate of inflation, how much would a video that you rented last year for $3.50 cost this year, if the rate of inflation was 4.3 percent?
8. Janetta has decided to donate half of what she earns to a neighborhood organization that helps the homeless. She is saving the other half to buy a car. What are the opportunity costs of her decision? What role do her values play in making this financial plan?
9. Why does compounding interest benefit someone who is saving money?
10. What are the two main reasons that people invest?

Student | Class | Instructor

Date Assigned | Date Completed

CHAPTER 1 Personal Financial Planning

Activity 1: *Attain Your Goals*

SCANS COMPETENCIES ACHIEVED

Allocating money, Creative thinking, Decision making, Problem solving, Self-management

OBJECTIVE: *Learn to set short-term goals and understand how personal spending and values impact goal setting.*

Writing down your personal financial goals can help you identify potential problems or opportunities that may come along. Write down your short-term financial goals in the space provided, and explain how you will achieve them.

Goals	Means

Student Class Instructor

Date Assigned Date Completed

CHAPTER 1 Personal Financial Planning

Activity 2: *Identify Your Financial Values*

SCANS COMPETENCIES ACHIEVED

Allocating money, Creative thinking, Decision making, Problem solving, Self-management

OBJECTIVE: *Determine how your values impact your financial decisions.*

As defined in the chapter, **values** are the beliefs and principles that you consider important, correct, and desirable. When deciding on financial goals, your values play a large part in what path you take. For instance, if your financial goals are to save for college, you might forego Saturday night pizza for a year (approximately $600) and put that money into a savings account instead. However, if you are simply crazy for pizza, and absolutely have to have it, then you may believe that pizza is a necessity and that the dollars spent on your weekly pies are worth the expense. How do your values impact your financial decisions? The following exercise will help you examine your own financial values.

Read the following scenario and then answer the questions.

> Suppose you received an inheritance of $200,000 from your Aunt Mildred. There are no restrictions on how you can spend the money, but you must use it for one thing only. How would you spend your inheritance? Some options are listed on the following page.

Rank each option from 1 to 6 with "1" being the most likely way you would use the money and "6" being the least likely way. At the right of each option is a corresponding value. There are no wrong answers.

Student ____________________ Class __________ Instructor __________

Date Assigned ____________________ Date Completed ____________________

Option	Rank	Value
A. Pay for the best college available.		A. Respect for knowledge and education
B. Put the money toward a large house in a fancy neighborhood.		B. Desire for home and personal security
C. Go on the biggest shopping spree of your life.		C. Desire for material possessions
D. Give the money away to charity.		D. Consideration for others and their welfare
E. Put all your money into savings for the future.		E. Concern for financial security
F. Purchase a business to manage.		F. Desire for power and authority

Based on your rankings of each financial option and the corresponding value, answer the questions below and on the following page.

Which value is the most important to you? Which is the least important? How have experiences at home, at school, and in your community influenced the way you ranked these two values?

List the items you ranked 1, 2, and 3 (the three you valued the most). Identify how you could make personal financial changes today to someday reach those financial goals.

1. ______________________________

2. ______________________________

3. ______________________________

Student ____________________ Class ____________ Instructor ____________

Date Assigned ____________________ Date Completed ____________________

CHAPTER 1 Personal Financial Planning

Math-Building Skills: Tracking Income and Expense

DIRECTIONS: *Once you have identified your short-term goals, keep track of all your income and spending for seven days. Use the form below.*

Beginning cash on hand $____________

Date	Source — INCOME	Amount
	Total Income	

Date	Item — EXPENSES	Amount
	Total Expenses	

Subtract your total expenses from your total income.

Ending cash on hand $____________.

Student	Class	Instructor
Date Assigned	Date Completed	

CHAPTER 1 Personal Financial Planning

Your Financial Portfolio Worksheet

Getting Your Own Wheels

Are you dreaming of buying your own car? Look in your local newspaper for a used car you would like to buy. How much will it cost? Suppose you could afford 25 percent of the total price for a down payment. How much money will you need to borrow to pay the complete cost of the car you want? Then calculate how much money you'll need for your monthly car payment.

	1 Year	2 Years	3 Years	4 Years
Cost of car	$______	______	______	______
25% down payment	$______	______	______	______
Amount of loan (Cost of car − 25% down payment)	$______	______	______	______
Interest factor	0.08698	0.04522	0.03133	0.02441
Monthly payment (Amount of loan × interest factor)	$______	______	______	______
Total amount paid for car (Monthly payment × number of months)	$______	______	______	______
Amount of interest paid (Total amount paid for car − amount of loan)	$______	______	______	______

Calculate what your monthly payment will be if you paid off your loan in 1, 2, 3, and 4 years.

____

1. What is the total amount you will pay for your car if you pay it off in 1, 2, 3, or 4 years?

____

2. How much interest will you pay on your loan if you pay it off in 1, 2, 3, or 4 years?

____

3. Which payment plan would enable you to pay the least amount of money for your car?

____

4. Which payment plan would have the lowest monthly payment?

____

Student Class Instructor

Date Assigned Date Completed

CHAPTER 1 Personal Financial Planning

Finance Online: Exploring Financial Planning

Throughout this workbook, you will discover how the personal financial planning industry is utilizing the Internet to meet your needs.

Developing a personal financial plan is an important part of the strategy to secure your future well-being. As you develop a plan, you will discover how inflation can affect your saving and investing strategy. For this activity use an Internet search engine to look for the inflation rate for the year you were born.

Keywords Used	Site Name	Web Site Addresses	Information Offered

1. How much was $100 of today's money worth the year you were born?

2. If you are working now, how much would your hourly wage have been worth that year? (If you are not working, use $6 per hour as an example.)

3. How much would the same wage have been worth 25, 50, and 100 years ago?

Student	Class	Instructor
Date Assigned	Date Completed	

CHAPTER 1 Personal Financial Planning

Software Activity (Optional)

Spreadsheet Application

Calculating and Analyzing Personal Investment Strategies

OBJECTIVE: *To illustrate the value of compounding and the importance of long-term saving and investment strategies.*

Practice Situation

The following data presents two investment strategies. For strategy 1, assume that Beverly contributes $1,000 annually to her investment account from age 18 through age 24. For strategy 2, Matt contributes $1,000 annually to his investment account beginning at age 28 through age 65. For each strategy presented, assume that the investment will generate an average rate of return of 10 percent per year. Calculate the future values for both investment strategies at age 65, then answer the questions that follow.

Strategy 1: Beverly				Strategy 2: Matt		
Age	Annual Contribution	Year-end Value		Age	Annual Contribution	Year-end Value
18	1,000			25	0	
19	1,000			26	0	
20	1,000			27	0	
21	1,000			28	1,000	
22	1,000			29	1,000	
23	1,000			30	1,000	
24	1,000			31	1,000	
64	0			64	1,000	
65	0			65	1,000	
	Summary Data:				*Summary Data:*	
	Principal Invested				Principal Invested	
	Future Value				Future Value	
	Investment Return				Investment Return	

Continue Spreadsheet data from years 25 through 63

Student ______ Class ______ Instructor ______

Date Assigned ______ Date Completed ______

Spreadsheet Directions

1. Start your spreadsheet software and open problem **SA01.xls.** Enter the data into the spreadsheet. For Strategy 1, invest $1,000 annually from age 18 to age 24. For years 25 through 65, the annual investment equals $0. In Strategy 2, do not invest anything until age 28. At this point, $1,000 is invested each year through retirement at age 65.
2. Input the formulas to calculate the following:
   - Year-end values
   - Total principal invested
   - Total future value
   - Return on investment

   Note: Format all dollar amounts to Currency, 2 decimals.
3. Perform the calculations, then save your work to a new file labeled **SA01***.xls.** (Replace *** with your initials.)
4. Print out a copy of your work if your teacher has instructed you to do so.

Interpreting Results

1. What is the *total investment* for each investment strategy?
2. What are the *future values* associated with each strategy?
3. Which strategy would generate the largest *return on investment* at age 65?

Drawing Conclusions

1. Based on your calculations, which investor has executed the more favorable investment strategy? Explain.

   ______

   ______
2. Why is it important for young adults to understand how to save, invest, and use money wisely?

   ______

   ______

Student Class Instructor

Date Assigned Date Completed

CHAPTER 1 Personal Financial Planning

SELF-ASSESSMENT QUIZ

DIRECTIONS: *Circle the letter of the choice that best completes the statement or answers the question.*

1. The trade-off when you make a choice is called (A) cost of choice (B) a financial goal (C) opportunity lost (D) opportunity cost.
2. Future value is (A) the amount to which your original deposit will increase based on a certain interest rate and a certain time (B) the gross national product forecasted over a ten-year period (C) the current interest rate (D) the result of supply and demand.
3. Inflation refers to (A) a balloon payment (B) a general rise in prices of goods and services (C) the rise in the price of a stock (D) the cost of intangible goods.
4. The ability to easily convert your financial resources into cash without loss in value is called (A) inflation (B) compounding (C) liquidity (D) present value.
5. A series of equal deposits is (A) serial deposits (B) an annuity (C) time deposits (D) annual deposits.
6. Present value is (A) the amount spent to provide someone with a gift (B) last year's inflation rate adjusted to today's dollar (C) the amount of money you need to deposit now to attain a desired future amount (D) the current value of a past investment.
7. Time value of money is best described as (A) an increase in an amount of money as a result of interest or dividends earned (B) what one hour of your time is worth in today's dollars (C) the current value of the dollar (D) the amount of work time needed to make up for inflation.
8. Which of the following is not part of the financial planning process? (A) Determining your current financial situation (B) Developing financial goals (C) Acquiring consumable and durable goods on credit (D) Identifying and evaluating alternative courses of action.
9. The term used to define the price that is paid for the use of another's money is (A) a price tag (B) money market value (C) interest (D) face value.
10. The amount that your original deposit will be worth on a specific date, based on a specific interest rate over a specific period of time, is called (A) present value (B) increased value (C) future value (D) dollar value.

Student Class Instructor

Date Assigned Date Completed

CHAPTER 2 Financial Aspects of Career Planning

Reviewing Key Terms: Complete the Sentence

DIRECTIONS: *Using terms from the following list, complete the sentences below. Write the letter of the term you have chosen in the space provided.*

A. career	D. demographic trends	G. informational interview
B. potential earning power	E. service industries	H. résumé
C. aptitudes	F. internship	I. cover letter
		J. mentor

1. ______ are ways in which groups of people change over time.

2. ______ is the amount of money you may earn over time.

3. An experienced employee who serves as a teacher and counselor for a less experienced person is called a(n) ______.

4. ______ provide services for a fee.

5. ______ is a position in which a person receives training by working with people who are experienced in a particular field.

6. ______ is a meeting with someone who works in your area of interest who can provide practical information about the career or company you are considering.

7. A one- or two-page summary of your education, training, experience, and qualifications is called a(n) ______.

8. The natural abilities that people possess are called ______.

9. A commitment to work in a field that you find interesting and fulfilling is called a(n) ______.

10. A(n) ______ is a personal letter that is presented to a potential employer with a résumé.

Student Class Instructor

Date Assigned Date Completed

CHAPTER 2 Financial Aspects of Career Planning

Understanding Key Concepts

DIRECTIONS: *On a separate sheet of paper, answer the questions below.*

1. Describe a trade-off you would be willing to make when choosing a career.
2. What should you know about to choose a career that will provide balance between personal and financial satisfaction?
3. List three major categories of factors that influence employment opportunities.
4. Which factor do you think influences employment opportunities the most? Explain your choice.
5. Identify four ways to obtain work-related experience.
6. Jack wants to prepare for a career that will not be obsolete by the time he graduates. Suggest an information source where he can find current information on the fastest-growing employment categories.
7. Camille has an appointment for a job interview. How can she make the most of the opportunity?
8. What factors can affect your beginning salary?
9. Clare applied for a job as a firefighter at an all-male fire department. The town council refused her application because the cost of building separate shower and sleep facilities was not in the budget. Clare wants to sue the township. Does she have a case? Explain your answer.
10. Richard snaps at his dog each weekday morning, experiences headaches at work, and has trouble sleeping at night. Explain why he might consider a job change.

Student	Class	Instructor
Date Assigned	Date Completed	

CHAPTER 2 Financial Aspects of Career Planning

Activity 1: *Evaluate Possible Career Choices*

SCANS COMPETENCIES ACHIEVED
Creative thinking, Problem solving, Self-management, Reasoning, Acquiring and evaluating information

OBJECTIVE: *Learn to evaluate positive and negative aspects of potential careers.*

Comparing and contrasting different career options can help you make an informed choice. Write down three careers that interest you. Then fill in the spaces with potential positives and negatives for each career.

Career	Positives	Negatives

Student _______________ Class _______________ Instructor _______________

Date Assigned _______________ Date Completed _______________

CHAPTER 2 Financial Aspects of Career Planning

Activity 2: *Analyze Your Career Goals*

SCANS COMPETENCIES ACHIEVED

Creative thinking, Problem solving, Self-management, Reasoning, Integrity/honesty

OBJECTIVE: *Determine and evaluate which factors are important to you in choosing a career.*

Is salary more important to you than job satisfaction? Are you more concerned with the hours you'll work or with the atmosphere you'll be working in? How critical are education benefits, day-care facilities, a pension plan, the opportunity to work with computers and technology, and the freedom to be your own boss? These are just a few of the many factors you'll have to consider when you start to think about what career to choose. The following exercise will help you figure out what is important to you and point you in the right direction on your career path.

Read through the following list of job-related items. If you feel some things are missing, add them on the blank lines. Then, assign each item a number from 1 to 5, with 1 being the most important to you and 5 the least important. Remember, there are no wrong answers, just personal preferences.

_____ Good pay

_____ Pleasant working conditions

_____ Convenient hours

_____ Long vacations

_____ Availability of day care and other family-friendly programs

_____ Good chance for training and education

_____ Informal, casual atmosphere

_____ High status

_____ Good job security

_____ Chance for advancement

_____ Opportunity to help people

_____ Good choice of health plans and other benefits

_____ Low-stress environment

_____ Opportunities to use my strongest skills

_____ Chance to work with what I really love

_____ Workplace close to home

_____ Chance to travel

_____ Diversity of employees

_____ Chance to work outdoors

_____ Interesting work that is never boring

____

____

____

____

Student ______________________ Class ______________ Instructor ______________

Date Assigned ______________________ Date Completed ______________________

Now, based on your rankings, answer the following questions.

1. Of the items you ranked highest (1), which one do you consider the most important? Why?

2. Of those items that you ranked lowest (5), which one do you consider the least important? Why?

3. Look at the items that received a 1, or the highest ranking. List some steps that you could take today to make it more likely that you'll someday have a career that will include the items that you consider important.

Student Class Instructor

Date Assigned Date Completed

CHAPTER 2 Financial Aspects of Career Planning

Math-Building Skills: Computing Compensation

Even if you're more interested in having a career that's fascinating, offers a chance to help people, or lets you travel all over the world, earning enough money to support your lifestyle—whatever it is—is still important. In this activity, you'll use your math skills to compare the incomes of three different careers.

DIRECTIONS: *Listed below are three jobs and their annual pay for this year. Assume that earnings will keep pace with inflation (3 percent a year) and be boosted by an additional 2 percent each year in raises. Then answer each question.*

Kindergarten teacher	$24,000
Computer programmer	$29,000
Auto assembly worker	$27,000

1. How much will the kindergarten teacher earn next year? ______

A. $24,480 C. $25,200

B. $24,720 D. $26,400

How did you calculate your answer?

______

______

2. In 10 years, the computer programmer's salary will be ______.

A. $47,237.94 C. $50,012.42

B. $48,000.00 D. $50,090.60

How did you calculate your answer?

______

______

3. The auto assembly worker receives an annual benefits package, including health insurance, tuition reimbursement, and free company-run day care, worth $4,000 a year. She has deducted from her paycheck $310 a year in union dues. How much will her total employment package be worth this year?

______

How did you calculate your answer?

______

______

Student _____ Class _____ Instructor _____

Date Assigned _____ Date Completed _____

CHAPTER 2 Financial Aspects of Career Planning

Your Financial Portfolio Worksheet

Applying for a Job

Before you interview for a job, you will probably have to fill out an application. Take time to practice "the art" of completing application forms. Always fill out a job application as neatly and accurately as possible. Write N/A in any blank for which an answer is not required. N/A means "Not Applicable" and tells the employer that you saw the question, but it does not apply to you. Fill out the application on the following page, being sure to fill it out completely. Use a pencil before you complete the application in ink or use a rough copy. Then complete the questions below.

Were there any questions that you could not answer? If so list the questions.

_____

_____

_____

_____

_____

_____

What do you think a neatly prepared application would tell a prospective employer about you?

_____

_____

_____

_____

_____

_____

_____

APPLICATION FOR EMPLOYMENT

SUPERIOR MARKETS

DIRECTIONS: Please use a pen and print.
Answer all sections completely and accurately.

NAME			SOCIAL SECURITY NUMBER
LAST	FIRST	MIDDLE	– –

HOME ADDRESS				
NUMBER	STREET	CITY	STATE	ZIP

TELEPHONE #	ALTERNATE #

POSITION APPLIED FOR	SPECIFY DAYS AND HOURS AVAILABLE	PAY DESIRED

EDUCATION	NAME AND ADDRESS OF SCHOOL	COURSE	DATE LEFT
MIDDLE SCHOOL			
HIGH SCHOOL			
VOCATIONAL SCHOOL			
COLLEGE OR UNIVERSITY			
OTHER			

LAST EMPLOYMENT				
NAME OF COMPANY	ADDRESS	SUPERVISOR	JOB	PAY
DATE BEGAN	DATE LEFT	REASON FOR LEAVING		

Additional qualifications applicant has to offer for consideration. These may include job-related interests, experiences, or volunteer activities.

____

____

____

____

____

The facts set forth on my application are true and complete.

DATE ______________________ SIGNATURE ______________________

Student Class Instructor

Date Assigned Date Completed

CHAPTER 2 Financial Aspects of Career Planning

Finance Online: Investigating Careers

Chapter 2 makes several suggestions for using the Internet to research careers and find employment.

In researching careers, you will want to find out about the goals of a profession. One good source to tell you about the goals and responsibilities of a profession is its professional associations. As you explore careers, you should consider using the Internet to find out about professional associations. For this activity, imagine you are interested in a career working with animals. Use an Internet search engine to look up veterinarian associations.

Keywords Used	Site Name	Web Site Addresses	Information Offered

1. Describe the goals of one of the veterinarian associations.

2. Does this association have any job listings on the Web site or its links? Write down the job title and salary from one listing.

3. Explore links to other professions that do not require a degree in veterinary medicine but are still related to the field. List three of these professions.

Student	Class	Instructor
Date Assigned	Date Completed	

CHAPTER 2 Financial Aspects of Career Planning

Software Activity (Optional)

Spreadsheet Application

Comparing Employment Offers

OBJECTIVE: *To calculate and analyze the monetary values of employee benefits and employment opportunities.*

Practice Situation

Ing Lee has been offered a job with two different companies. Job 1 offers a salary of $45,200, a one-time sign-on bonus of $2,000, and nontaxable employee benefits of $4,000. Job 2 will pay a salary of $47,000 and $6,100 of nontaxable benefits. Job 2 will also require a move to another city where the cost of living is 2% higher than that of the Job 1 location. The employer that has offered Job 2 is willing to pay for moving expenses. Job 1 offers annual raises of 8 percent, while Job 2 offers annual raises of 3 percent. Compute the monetary values of both job offers for the next 2 years, then answer the questions that follow. Use a 28% tax rate.

Year One Monetary Value	Job 1	Job 2
Salary		
Bonus		
Tax equivalent value of nontaxable benefits		
Less: Cost of Living Adjustment		
Year One Monetary Value		

Year Two Monetary Value	Job 1	Job 2
Salary		
Bonus		
Tax equivalent value of nontaxable benefits		
Less: Cost of Living Adjustment		
Year Two Monetary Value		

Summary Information	Job 1	Job 2
Years One & Two Monetary Value		

Student Class Instructor

Date Assigned Date Completed

Spreadsheet Directions

1. Start your spreadsheet software and open problem **SA02.xls.** For year one, enter the salary figures for both job opportunities into the spreadsheet. Next, enter the bonus amount for Job 1.
2. Input the formulas to calculate the tax equivalent value for the nontaxable benefits for both jobs.
3. Input the formula to calculate the cost of living adjustment for Job 2. Hint: a higher cost of living will mean a deduction to the monetary value of the job offer.
4. Input the formulas to calculate the total monetary value for each job option for the first year. *Note: Format all dollar amounts to Currency, 2 decimals.*
5. Next complete the spreadsheet for Year Two. Input the formulas to calculate the new salary figures accounting for the annual raise.
6. Enter the formulas (or copy the formulas from the spreadsheet you just completed) to calculate the tax equivalent value for the nontaxable benefits for both jobs.
7. Enter the formula to calculate the cost of living adjustment based on the new salary amount for Job 2.
8. Calculate the totals for both jobs for year two.
9. Save your work to a new file labeled **SA02***.xls.** (Replace *** with your initials.)
10. Print out a copy of your work if your teacher has instructed you to do so.

Interpreting Results

1. What is the monetary value for both job opportunities in year one?

___

2. What is the monetary value for both job opportunities in year two?

___

3. What is the cumulative monetary value for each job at the end of year two?

___

Drawing Conclusions

1. If you plan to work in the job that you accept for at least two years, which opportunity would be the favorable choice based only on financial concerns? Explain.

___

___

2. Aside from financial implications, what other issues should be considered when comparing two job opportunities?

___

___

___

___

Student Class Instructor

Date Assigned Date Completed

CHAPTER 2 Financial Aspects of Career Planning

SELF-ASSESSMENT QUIZ

DIRECTIONS: *Circle the letter of the choice that best completes the statement or answers the question.*

1. Having a college degree increases your (A) ability to work well with others (B) conflicts with employers (C) creativity in solving problems (D) potential earning power.
2. What do aptitude tests do? (A) match your interests with various kinds of work (B) decide the ideal career for you (C) assess your performance on the job (D) test your understanding of demographic trends.
3. More working parents most likely expands the supply of jobs in (A) health care (B) physical fitness (C) food services (D) travel services.
4. Which of the following factors may cause a decrease in career opportunities? (A) more working parents (B) high interest rates (C) more leisure time (D) increased demand for goods and services.
5. An example of a job in a service industry is a(n) (A) garment worker (B) automaker (C) physical therapist (D) wheat farmer.
6. Building houses with Habitat for Humanity is an example of (A) an internship (B) volunteer work (C) part-time employment (D) a class project.
7. Avoid employment agencies that charge a fee (A) from whoever hires you (B) from you after placing you (C) from you without delivering a job (D) that you split with your new employer.
8. A chronological résumé works best for job hunters who (A) have continuous work experience (B) have just graduated (C) are changing careers (D) want to highlight their skills.
9. While waiting to hear the results of an interview, you should send the interviewer a (A) résumé (B) cover letter (C) thank-you note (D) job acceptance.
10. An example of a tax-deferred benefit is (A) life insurance (B) health insurance (C) child-care services (D) a 401(k) plan.

Student ____________________ Class ____________ Instructor ____________

Date Assigned ____________________ Date Completed ____________________

CHAPTER 3 Money Management Strategy

Reviewing Key Terms: Complete the Sentence

DIRECTIONS: *Using terms from the following list, complete the sentences below. Write the letter of the term you have chosen in the space provided.*

A. money management	D. assets	G. insolvency
B. safe-deposit box	E. market value	H. cash flow
C. net worth	F. liabilities	I. budget
		J. consumer price index

1. ______ are any items of value that you own, including cash, property, personal possessions, and investments.

2. ______ are the debts you owe.

3. The difference between the amount you own and the debts you owe is called ______.

4. The method of planning how to get the most from your money is called ______.

5. A(n) ______ is a plan for using your money in a way that best meets your wants and needs.

6. ______ is the money that actually goes into and out of your wallet and bank accounts.

7. The price at which property could be sold is called its ______.

8. A(n) ______ is a small, secure storage compartment that can be rented in a bank.

9. A measure of the changes in prices for commonly purchased goods and services in the United States is called the ______.

10. ______ is the condition that occurs when a person's liabilities are greater than his or her assets.

Student | Class | Instructor

Date Assigned | Date Completed

CHAPTER 3 Money Management Strategy

Understanding Key Concepts

DIRECTIONS: On a separate sheet of paper, answer the questions below.

1. Identify two kinds of personal financial documents.
2. List three ways that organizing financial documents can help you.
3. Describe a balance sheet.
4. How do real estate and liquid assets differ?
5. Washington has an extensive collection of baseball cards. He wants to know how much his mint condition, rookie-year Hank Aaron is worth. How might he determine the card's current market value?
6. What kind of assets do people typically set aside for long-term financial needs?
7. Rachel's take-home pay is $600 per month. She pays $200 for rent and utilities, $100 for food, $5 for medication, and $30 for transportation. How much discretionary income does Rachel have?
8. Summarize the seven steps for creating a good budget.
9. Name four characteristics of a successful budget.
10. Cody is a freelance photographer who is paid only after he completes an assignment. He may spend several months working on a large, well-paying assignment or get many small jobs for less pay over the same period of time. Often he has to wait several weeks after completing a job for his paycheck. Which method of saving described in the chapter would you recommend for Cody? Explain why the other methods might not work for him.

Student ____________________ Class ____________ Instructor ____________

Date Assigned ____________________ Date Completed ____________________

CHAPTER 3 Money Management Strategy

Activity 1: *Prepare a Handout for Younger Students*

SCANS COMPETENCIES ACHIEVED
Writing, Teaching others, Creative thinking, Problem solving, Reasoning, Acquiring and evaluating information, Interpreting and communicating information, Organizing and maintaining information

OBJECTIVE: *Prepare a top ten list for sixth-graders of suggestions on how to become financially responsible.*

Sometimes the best way to understand an idea is to teach it to someone else. Imagine that you have been asked to make a short presentation to a group of sixth-graders on the topic of becoming financially responsible. As a handout, you have decided to give them a "top ten" countdown style list of things to do. Using the information in this chapter, make a list of financial suggestions with number 1 being the most important. Use a separate piece of paper to make notes and organize your choices.

10. ____________________

9. ____________________

8. ____________________

7. ____________________

6. ____________________

5. ____________________

4. ____________________

3. ____________________

2. ____________________

1. ____________________

Student Class Instructor

Date Assigned Date Completed

CHAPTER 3 Money Management Strategy

Activity 2: *Evaluate Personal Financial Statements*

SCANS COMPETENCIES ACHIEVED
Math, Reading, Problem solving, Reasoning, Acquiring and evaluating information, Interpreting and communicating information, Organizing and maintaining information

OBJECTIVE: *Analyze and correct personal financial statements.*

A friend has asked you to take a look at her personal financial statements to point out possible mistakes. Unfortunately, her statements contain eight errors, including items in the wrong categories, math mistakes, and incorrect understanding of cash flow. On the next page rewrite the statements using the same basic form, correcting the eight errors.

Balance Sheet

Liquid assets	
savings account	$ 900
½ ownership of car	1,200
Personal possessions	
stereo	600
snowboard	300
flute	250
clothing	875
Liabilities	
owed to parents for loan to buy car	(800)
monthly pledge to Habitat for Humanity	(20)
Net worth	$4,305

Cash Flow Statement

Cash flow, current month	
Income	
take-home pay from job at grocery store	$ 325
allowance	75
baby-sitting	60
interest on savings account at 4% per year	36
total	496
Expenses	
gas for car	(35)
lunches at school, about $15 per week	
entertainment	(60)
car insurance	(50)
deposit to savings	(100)
total	$ (260)
Total Cash Flow	$ 236

Student Class Instructor

Date Assigned Date Completed

Student _______________ Class _______________ Instructor _______________

Date Assigned _______________ Date Completed _______________

CHAPTER 3 Money Management Strategy

Math-Building Skills: Conducting a Survey

Different people have different skill levels when it comes to budgeting, keeping track of income and expenses, and staying up-to-date with their financial record-keeping.

DIRECTIONS: *To get an idea of how your classmates or friends are doing, create a personal finance survey that includes questions on different aspects of personal finance that you learned about in this chapter. The kinds of questions you might want to ask include, "Do you usually have a positive cash flow?" "How well do you keep track of income and expenses?" "What percentage of your income do you save? What percentage do you spend?" Be prepared to explain terms you use in the survey questions. Be careful NOT to ask about specific amounts of money, salary, and other sensitive or personal subjects. You can either hand out copies of your survey or interview people and write down their responses.*

When you have collected at least six completed surveys, tabulate your answers. Report the combined results in percentages on the lines below. If necessary, review the procedure for finding percentages in the Math Skills Builder *appendix of your textbook. Share your results with the class.*

Student | Class | Instructor

Date Assigned | Date Completed

CHAPTER 3 Money Management Strategy

Your Financial Portfolio Worksheet

What Is Your Net Worth?

Calculate your net worth. List all your liquid assets, personal possessions, and any other assets, as well as liabilities (what you owe).

Fill in the areas in the following chart that are applicable and list others that apply to you.

LIQUID ASSETS		
Checking account balance		
Savings accounts		
Other		
PERSONAL POSSESSIONS		
INVESTMENT ASSETS		
Total Assets		
LIABILITIES		
Total Liabilities		
Net Worth (assets − liabilities)		

Are you surprised that your net worth is as much (or as little) as it is? How much would you like your net worth to be in 10 years? When you retire?

Student ____________ Class ____________ Instructor ____________

Date Assigned ____________ Date Completed ____________

CHAPTER 3 Money Management Strategy

Finance Online: Using the Consumer Price Index

Chapter 3 discusses the Consumer Price Index (CPI) as an aid in determining whether you are spending too much for commonly purchased goods and services.

The Bureau of Labor Statistics compiles facts about the average expenses for Americans that could help you. For instance, is your family overspending on entertainment with money that might go toward the shoes or jacket you've been asking for? To find out, consult the Consumer Price Index. For this activity use an Internet search engine to find the Consumer Price Index for All Urban Customers.

Keywords Used	Site Name	Web Site Addresses	Information Offered

1. Is the Consumer Price Index increasing or decreasing?

____

____

2. What percentage of consumers' incomes goes for food? Apparel? Recreation?

____

____

3. Keep track of your food, apparel, and recreation expenses for a month. Collect all sales receipts, add the amounts in each category, and divide the total by your monthly take-home income. How do your results compare to the percentages from the Consumer Price Index?

____

____

Student ______ Class ______ Instructor ______

Date Assigned ______ Date Completed ______

CHAPTER 3 Money Management Strategy

Software Activity (Optional)

Quicken Application

Preparing and Evaluating a Budget

OBJECTIVE: *To create a budget, determine budget variances, and implement a successful money management strategy.*

Practice Situation

Hannah Peck would like to create a budget for the month of March. She estimates the following income and expense data for the month.

Budget Data:

Salary $1,875	Car Payment $190	Doctor visits $60
Rent $500	Utility bills $110	Entertainment $70
Car Insurance $105	Clothing $250	Groceries $300
Household $45	Eating Out $80	Auto fuel $45
Emergency savings transfer $50	Long-term savings transfer $100	Interest income $30

Actual Data:

Hannah entered her banking activities into Quicken. She recorded the deposit of her paycheck of $1,875. She spent $287.76 on clothes, $260.88 on groceries, $96.88 for utilities. She also visited her eye doctor and paid her $80 and $25 for a prescription. She spent $120 on entertainment and $100 at restaurants. She bought new dishes at Crate & Barrel for $58.65. She earned $27.88 in interest on each of her savings accounts. Her car insurance was $107 this month. Auto gas was $54.50. Her other expenses were paid as budgeted. She made her planned transfers into her savings accounts.

Using Quicken, record Hannah's budgeted income and expenses. Then, use Quicken's Reports to generate a Monthly Budget Report for March. Quicken will use Hannah's actual expenditures and the budgeted amounts to create this report.

Quicken Directions

1. Start your Quicken software program and open the file **SA03.qdf.**
2. Select *Budget* from the **Planning** menu.
3. Click the **Income** tab and highlight the income account for which you will create a budget.
4. Under the account budget section to your right, click on *Monthly Detail.*
5. You will notice zero amounts underneath each month for this account. Click on the zero amount and change it to the budgeted amount. Enter this amount in the March column. Click **Apply**. Input the income amounts, then the expenses by clicking the **Expenses** tab. Use only whole dollar amounts.

6. As you enter each budget amount for March, notice *Total Income, Total Expenses,* and *Difference* at the bottom of your screen. If all of Hannah's budgeted amounts are correct, the *Difference* amount will equal $0.00. Check your entries if the *Difference* does not equal $0.00.
7. When the *Difference* amount is equal to $0.00, print Hannah's budget. Click **Print** in the top of the Budget window. Use this report to answer questions that follow.
8. Generate a Monthly Budget Report. Select *Monthly Budget Report* from the **Reports** menu in the Budget window.
9. Click **Customize** and enter the custom dates from 3/1/06 to 3/31/06.
10. Click on the **Accounts** tab to verify that Hannah's checking account is the only account checked. Uncheck Hannah's savings accounts if they are marked. Click **OK**.
11. Print this report. Click **Print** in the top menu of the Monthly Budget window. You will use this report to answer the questions that follow.
12. To save your work, click **File** in the top menu, then select *File Operations,* then *Copy.* In the *Name* field, enter **SA03***.qdf.** (Replace *** with your initials.) In the Location field, enter **A:** to save your data file to a floppy disk.
13. Close your Quicken software program.

Interpreting Results

1. What total amount was budgeted in March for discretionary expenses? Mandatory expenses?

____

2. In which categories did Hannah overspend in the month of March?

____

____

3. What was the Overall Total Difference between Actual and Budget on the Monthly Budget Report?

____

Drawing Conclusions

1. Did Hannah stay within her budget for March? Explain.

____

____

2. Are Hannah's budgeted amounts realistic? How would you suggest that she adjust her budget?

____

____

____

Student Class Instructor

Date Assigned Date Completed

CHAPTER 3 Money Management Strategy

SELF-ASSESSMENT QUIZ

DIRECTIONS: *Circle the letter of the choice that best completes the statement or answers the question.*

1. An opportunity cost is a(n) (A) good price (B) trade-off (C) income (D) asset.
2. A home file is the best place to keep (A) valuable collectibles (B) birth certificates (C) mortgage papers (D) canceled checks.
3. Your net worth is the difference between your (A) liquid assets and your real estate's market value (B) personal possessions' market value and your investment assets (C) assets and liabilities (D) current liabilities and long-term liabilities.
4. Cars fall into the category of (A) liquid assets (B) personal possessions (C) real estate (D) investment assets.
5. The condition that occurs when a person's liabilities are greater than his or her assets is called (A) long-term liability (B) low cash flow (C) insolvency (D) bankruptcy.
6. An example of cash outflow is (A) a paycheck (B) an allowance (C) interest on savings (D) a credit card payment.
7. The amount of income left after taxes and other deductions are taken out of your paycheck is called (A) net pay (B) gross pay (C) discretionary income (D) cash flow.
8. An example of a variable expense is (A) a mortgage payment (B) an auto insurance premium (C) school tuition (D) medical expenses.
9. Your budget shows a surplus when you (A) spend more money than budgeted on entertainment (B) receive a cut in pay (C) spend money budgeted for emergencies on car repairs (D) spend less than you earn.
10. The key to establishing a sound financial future is to (A) increase your savings (B) keep track of every expense (C) buy whatever you want (D) run a budget deficit.

Student Class Instructor

Date Assigned Date Completed

CHAPTER 4 Consumer Purchasing Strategies and Legal Protection

Reviewing Key Terms: Complete the Sentence

DIRECTIONS: *Using terms from the following list, complete the sentences below. Write the letter of the term you have chosen in the space provided.*

A. cooperative	D. warranty	G. mediation
B. impulse buying	E. service contract	H. arbitration
C. open dating	F. fraud	I. small claims court
		J. class-action suit

1. ______ is the attempt by a neutral third party to resolve a conflict between a customer and a business through discussion and negotiation.
2. ______ means purchasing items on the spur of the moment.
3. The process where a conflict between a customer and a business is resolved by an impartial third party whose decision is legally binding is called ______.
4. ______ deals with legal disputes involving amounts below a certain limit.
5. ______ is a dishonest business practice that is meant to deceive, trick, or gain an unfair advantage.
6. ______ describes the freshness or "shelf life" of a perishable product, such as bread or milk.
7. A separately purchased agreement by the manufacturer or distributor to cover the repair costs of the item is called a(n) ______.
8. A(n) ______ is a written guarantee from the manufacturer or distributor that specifies the conditions under which the product can be returned, replaced, or repaired.
9. A nonprofit organization owned and operated by its members is called a(n) ______.
10. A(n) ______ is a legal claim on behalf of all the people who have suffered the same injustice.

Student | Class | Instructor

Date Assigned | Date Completed

CHAPTER 4 Consumer Purchasing Strategies and Legal Protection

Understanding Key Concepts

DIRECTIONS: *On a separate sheet of paper, answer the questions below.*

1. Identify two factors that might affect your purchase of a pair of running shoes.
2. Name five sources of product information that you might consult before making an expensive purchase.
3. Brian has $3,000 to spend on a laptop computer. He has narrowed his choices to the latest model with lots of speed and memory for $2,999 or a slower, discontinued model with half the memory for only $1,500. Which would you recommend he purchase? Explain your answer.
4. Compare the advantages and disadvantages of using cash instead of credit to purchase an expensive item.
5. Imagine you are buying a new guitar. Describe how you would make the purchase using the research-based approach from Section 1.
6. Calculate the unit price for a 24-ounce bag of candy that costs $3.20.
7. In what order should you pursue the following courses of action when you are dissatisfied with a purchase and suspect fraud? (a) resort to dispute resolution (b) take legal action (c) return to the place of purchase (d) get help from a consumer agency (e) contact company headquarters?
8. Whom can you call to find out about dispute resolution programs?
9. Paul recently purchased a home in a newly built subdivision. He discovered that toxic waste from a nearby factory had seeped into his backyard soil and was killing his plants and the wild animals that visited his yard. He noticed the plants in his neighbors' yards were also dying. He has complained to the builder and factory manager, written to the corporate office of both, tried to set up a dispute resolution, but the problem persists. What legal action would you recommend to Paul? Explain your answer.
10. What is a legal aid society?

Student | Class | Instructor
Date Assigned | Date Completed

CHAPTER 4 Consumer Purchasing Strategies and Legal Protection

Activity 1: *Comparison Shopping*

SCANS COMPETENCIES ACHIEVED

Reading, Writing, Math, Reasoning, Problem solving, Decision making, Allocating money, Acquiring and evaluating information, Interpreting and communicating information

OBJECTIVE: *Compare the price and quality of national and store brands on several different products.*

Are you the kind of person who always likes to buy the better known national brands? Or do you feel that in-house store brands are just as good—and cheaper? In this activity, you'll get a chance to compare several items in terms of price and quality.

In groups of three, go to a grocery store, drugstore, or discount store. Choose three different kinds of items that you regularly use. For example, you might choose shampoo, chocolate cookies, and dish detergent; or applesauce, orange juice, and skin lotion. Buy a national brand and an in-house store version of each kind of product. After each one in your group tries the products, use the chart below to evaluate them. In the last row, make a judgment on which product offers better value for the money.

Product	Price	Unit Price (if applicable)	Evaluation

Student ______ Class ______ Instructor ______

Date Assigned ______ Date Completed ______

CHAPTER 4 Consumer Purchasing Strategies and Legal Protection

Activity 2: *Using a Research-Based Approach to Buying*

SCANS COMPETENCIES ACHIEVED

Reading, Writing, Decision making, Problem solving, Knowing how to learn, Acquiring and evaluating information, Organizing and maintaining information

OBJECTIVE: *Follow a research-based procedure for making a major purchase.*

Following a research-based approach to make a purchase can help you feel confident that you're making the best buying decision. In this activity, you will identify an actual need you have for a product, gather information to better understand the need and the product, and learn about the marketplace in which you will make the purchase.

1. Identifying Your Need

What do you want to buy?

______

______

______

Why do you feel you need it?

______

______

______

What are other options instead of purchasing this item?

______

______

______

Are any of the alternatives to purchasing acceptable? Explain. If not, go on to section 2.

______

______

______

Student Class Instructor

Date Assigned Date Completed

2. Gathering Information

List prices, availability, advantages, disadvantages, and other information about three different brands or versions of your item. Note the sources of the information.

What special features do you want in the item?

If the price is too high, what compromises are you willing to make?

Where are some places you can buy the item?

Which payment option is the best? Why?

What are some ways you can pay for the item?

Which payment option is the best? Why?

Can you take advantage of sales, special warranties, or other discounts? How?

3. Making Your Purchase Decision

After considering all the information, which option seems most appealing to you? Why?

Student Class Instructor

Date Assigned Date Completed

CHAPTER 4 Consumer Purchasing Strategies and Legal Protection

Math-Building Skills: Cash or Credit?

Your sister has decided to buy a new snowboard. The one she wants costs $275, including sales tax, at a local sporting goods store.

She is not sure of the best way to pay for her snowboard. She could pay cash; she has $450 in a savings account that pays 2% a year in interest. If she paid cash, it would take her six months to put the $275 back in her savings account. She could also use her credit card, which charges 18% interest a year. If she used her credit card, it would take her six months to pay off her bill. She has asked you to help her figure out the better way to pay for her snowboard.

DIRECTIONS: *Using your math skills, analyze the total costs of the two purchasing options and make a recommendation. Use the space below to make calculations. Then write your recommendation and explain your reasoning on the lines.*

Student | Class | Instructor

Date Assigned | Date Completed

CHAPTER 4 Consumer Purchasing Strategies and Legal Protection

Your Financial Portfolio Worksheet

Consumer Purchasing Strategies and Legal Protection

Better Budget

What is your budget? A budget can help you see where you are spending your money and assist you in determining how long it will take to save for a special purchase. On the budget worksheet below calculate your income and expenses for one month.

INCOME	Average Monthly Income
Total Income	
EXPENSES BY TYPE	**Average Monthly Amount**
Fixed Expenses	
Variable Expenses	
Total Expenses	

Student ______ Class ______ Instructor ______

Date Assigned ______ Date Completed ______

What is your total income? ______

What are your total expenses? ______

What can you save each month?
(income − expenses) ______

What is the cost of your desired purchase? ______

How long will it take you to save for what you want? ______

Student ________________ Class ________ Instructor ________

Date Assigned ________________ Date Completed ________________

CHAPTER 4 Consumer Purchasing Strategies and Legal Protection

Finance Online: Gathering Information

Chapter 4 recommends that you research alternatives before making an expensive purchase. One good source for this research is the Internet.

The most expensive purchase you are likely to make in the near future is a vehicle. Which vehicle model appeals to you most? You probably know how the vehicle looks, but what else do you know about it? Try researching your favorite vehicle and gathering information that can help you make comparisons with other models or different versions of the same model. For this activity use an Internet search engine to look up facts about a specific make and model. Try to find one Web site by the manufacturer and one by a consumer group or publication.

Keywords Used	Site Name	Web Site Addresses	Information Offered

1. Which make and model of vehicle did you choose to research?

____

2. List the following specifications for the car: acceleration, maximum speed, seating capacity, and gas mileage.

____

____

3. Based on your information, would you buy this car? Why or why not?

____

____

____

Student | Class | Instructor

Date Assigned | Date Completed

CHAPTER 4 Consumer Purchasing Strategies and Legal Protection

Software Activity (Optional)

Spreadsheet Application

Comparing Consumer Purchase Alternatives

OBJECTIVE: *To assess and compare the financial implications of purchase options.*

Practice Situation

Megan plans to buy a new mountain bike and must evaluate the following purchase options. Cycle Tech Bike Shop is offering the model that Megan likes for $289. The price includes a 6-month standard warranty. The clerk has recommended that she purchase an extended warranty for $40. The extended warranty will cover any repairs on her purchase for an additional 6 months. Megan likes the idea of the extended warranty because she knows this will protect her from unexpected repair costs.

Ann's Bike Shop is selling the same model for 10% off the tag price of $330. A 6-month standard warranty is also included in the price at Ann's, but they do not offer an extended warranty plan. Megan estimates that she would spend no more than $40 on repairs from month 7 through 12 after the purchase.

Megan also needs to purchase a helmet. Ann's Bike Shop has offered to throw in the helmet at no cost if Megan buys the bike from them. The helmet sells for $32 in both shops.

Use a sales tax rate of 8.5 percent and compare the purchase options. Answer the questions that follow.

	Cycle Tech Bike Shop	Ann's Bike Shop
Cost of mountain bike		
Extended warranty price		
Helmet		
Subtotal		
Sales Tax		
Total Purchase		
Repairs during the first year		
Total Cost		

Spreadsheet Directions

1. Start your spreadsheet software program and open problem **SA04.xls.**
2. Use the data listed above to complete the total cost of the purchase from Cycle Tech Bike Shop. Format all dollar amounts to Currency, 2 decimals. Insert formulas to calculate Subtotal, Sales Tax, Total Purchase, and Total Cost.
3. Record the costs associated with the purchase of the bike at Ann's Bike Shop. Insert the formula to calculate the cost of the mountain bike less the discount offered. Then, insert the formulas for Subtotal, Sales Tax, Total Purchase, and Total Cost.
4. Perform your calculations and complete the spreadsheet, then save your work to a new file labeled **SA04***.xls.** (Replace *** with your initials.)
5. Print out a copy of your work if your teacher has instructed you to do so.

Interpreting Results

1. What is the Total Cost of the purchase from Cycle Tech Bike Shop? ____________________
2. If Megan's estimate for repairs from month 7 through month 12 on the bike were correct, what is the Total Cost of the purchase from Ann's Bike Shop? ____________________

Drawing Conclusions

1. Based on your calculations, which bike shop is offering the best value to Megan on her desired purchase? Explain.

____

____

____

2. What financial risks or benefits can you identify that Megan should consider in her decision? What nonfinancial risks or benefits should Megan consider?

____

____

____

____

____

Student _______________ Class _______________ Instructor _______________

Date Assigned _______________ Date Completed _______________

CHAPTER 4 Consumer Purchasing Strategies and Legal Protection

SELF-ASSESSMENT QUIZ

DIRECTIONS: *Circle the letter of the choice that best completes the statement or answers the question.*

1. Social factors obviously affected Fran's choice of backpack if the pack is (A) a popular style (B) well-made (C) easily repaired (D) reasonably priced.

2. Before you begin to shop, you should (A) decide to pay cash (B) opt to delay payment (C) identify your needs (D) compare prices at different stores.

3. Comparison shopping is a waste of time when buying an item such as (A) a computer (B) shampoo (C) salt (D) school supplies.

4. You would most likely negotiate the price for a(n) (A) pair of jeans (B) airline ticket (C) tennis racket (D) car.

5. Direct selling includes all the following kinds of shopping EXCEPT (A) mail order (B) telephone sales (C) mall (D) online.

6. Product labels for appliances generally include (A) open dating (B) operating instructions (C) health claims (D) unit pricing.

7. An implied warranty guarantees that (A) a product is fit for its intended use (B) a defective product will be fixed (C) only certain parts of a product are under warranty (D) the distributor will replace a defective product.

8. When you are dissatisfied with a product and are seeking satisfaction, your last resort should be (A) complaining at the original place of purchase (B) getting help from a consumer agency (C) taking legal action in small claims court (D) using a dispute resolution program.

9. The settlement of a difference by a third party whose decision is legally binding is called (A) mediation (B) arbitration (C) dispute resolution (D) a class action.

10. A disagreement over an amount less than $500 is generally handled (A) through a legal aid society (B) in a class-action suit (C) at small claims court (D) by members of the American Bar Association.

Student Class Instructor

Date Assigned Date Completed

CHAPTER 5 Banking

Reviewing Key Terms: Complete the Sentence

DIRECTIONS: *Using terms from the following list, complete the sentences below. Write the letter of the term you have chosen in the space provided.*

A. automated teller machine	D. certificate of deposit	G. overdraft protection
B. debit card	E. rate of return	H. stop-payment order
C. credit union	F. compounding	I. endorsement
		J. bank reconciliation

1. A(n) ______ is a savings alternative that requires you to leave your money in a financial institution for a stated time period to earn a specific rate of return.
2. ______ is the process in which interest is earned on both the principal and on any previously earned interest.
3. The percentage of increase in the value of your savings from earned interest is called the ______.
4. A(n) ______ is a computer terminal that can be used to deposit, withdraw, and transfer money in your bank accounts.
5. ______ is an automatic loan made to you by a financial institution if you write a check for more money than you have in your account.
6. A(n) ______ is the signature of the party to whom a check has been written.
7. A request that an institution not cash a particular check is called a(n) ______.
8. A(n) ______ is a nonprofit financial institution that is owned by its members and organized for their benefit.
9. A report that accounts for the differences between the bank statement and your checkbook balance is called a(n) ______.
10. In a point-of-sale transaction, you can use a(n) ______ to purchase an item or a service at a retail store, in a restaurant, or elsewhere.

Student Class Instructor

Date Assigned Date Completed

CHAPTER 5 Banking

Understanding Key Concepts

DIRECTIONS: *On a separate sheet of paper, answer the questions below.*

1. Contrast commercial banks, credit unions, and investment companies. What different services do they offer? What makes each unique?
2. Explain the difference between a time deposit and a demand deposit.
3. Jamie applied for direct deposit of her paycheck. What will she receive on payday?
4. What can Dan do to prevent others from making withdrawals from his account if his debit card is stolen?
5. Why is your money safer in an institution that participates in the FDIC program?
6. Carly just received her first weekly paycheck for \$100. She plans to spend about \$50 a week on lunches, entertainment, and clothing but also wants to begin saving for when she goes to college in two years. Which savings program—a savings account, a certificate of deposit, a money market account, or a U.S. Savings Bond—should she use? Why?
7. Dirk opened up a savings account with \$600. At a yearly interest rate of 5 percent that is compounded monthly, how much interest will Dirk earn in six months?
8. Paloma has a savings account with an annual rate of return of 5.25 percent. She was planning to deposit all her savings in a certificate of deposit for two years at an annual rate of return of 7 percent. However, she just read that inflation is 10% and rising. What would you advise Paloma to do? Explain why.
9. Herman wants to earn interest on the money in his checking account but overdrafts his present account at least once a month. Why would you advise against his changing over to an interest-earning account that requires a minimum balance?
10. Put the following steps used in a bank reconciliation form in the correct order: (a) Subtract fees and charges listed on the statement from your checkbook balance. (b) Add the amounts of recent deposits not on the bank statement to the bank statement balance. (c) Subtract the total amount of outstanding checks from the balance on the bank statement. (d) Add any interest earned to your checkbook balance.

Student Class Instructor

Date Assigned Date Completed

CHAPTER 5 Banking

Activity 1: *Interview Relatives about Banking Choices*

SCANS COMPETENCIES ACHIEVED

Writing, Listening, Reasoning, Organizing and maintaining information, Interpreting and communicating information, Acquiring and evaluating information

OBJECTIVE: *Collect and analyze information about relatives' choice and use of banking services.*

As you learned in this chapter, the variety and choice of banking services available today is vast. It takes some work to gain enough understanding to make the right choices. One of the best sources of information is your relatives. They've had experience choosing and using banking services. This activity will help you take advantage of their knowledge.

Prepare a short questionnaire about banking services to give to three adults you know who have been bank customers for several years. Examining the chapter, figure out the most important questions to ask. Questions you might want to include are:

- What services do you consider most important?
- What advice would you offer to beginning consumers of banking services?
- Is there anything you'd like to warn against?
- What special tips can you share?

Use a separate sheet of paper to make notes on your questionnaire. Then prepare several copies of the final questions, distribute them to your interviewees, organize and evaluate the information you collect, and share your results with the class.

Student Class Instructor

Date Assigned Date Completed

CHAPTER 5 Banking

Activity 2: *Saving for College*

SCANS COMPETENCIES ACHIEVED

Decision making, Reasoning, Allocating money, Acquiring and evaluating information, Participating as a member of a team, Negotiating to arrive at a decision

OBJECTIVE: *Compare different savings programs.*

In two years, you will be starting college. You have managed to save $2,000 from your after-school job, but you have been hiding it under your mattress. Recently, you've decided to invest your savings so that you can earn interest on it. Which type of savings program will help you save the most for college?

Divide into groups of four. Each group member should research one type of savings program: a savings account, a CD, a money market account, or a U.S. Savings Bond. Conduct your research by visiting a financial institution in your area, by searching the Internet, or by looking at the financial section in your newspaper. Then, as a group, compare the different programs and decide which one would be the best way to invest your money. Fill in the chart on the following page, then answer the questions below.

Which type of savings would be your best option? Why?

Student Class Instructor

Date Assigned Date Completed

CHAPTER 5 Banking

	Savings Account	CD	Money Market	U.S. Savings Bond
Name				
Date of return				
How is interest compounded?				
Fees				
Restrictions				
Tax considerations				

Student ____________________ Class ____________ Instructor ____________

Date Assigned ____________________ Date Completed ____________________

CHAPTER 5 Banking

Math-Building Skills: Doing a Bank Reconciliation

It is March 31, and you just requested your checking account balance from an ATM. As frequently happens, the bank says you have a different amount than you think you should. The ATM says you have $234.01 in your account, but your register says you have $391.94. The mini-statement also tells you that all checks except #569 have cleared and that yesterday's deposit has not yet been credited to your account. You need to do a bank reconciliation to find out what your real balance is and whether it was you or your bank that made the errors.

DIRECTIONS: *Check the math on your check register and then answer the questions below. Keep in mind that you pay $8.50 every month for your checking services, your bank charges you $.50 for each ATM transaction, and you earn no interest on your account.*

MARCH

Date	Check Number		Amount	Balance
3/1				323.65
3/4	566	Pledge/World Wildlife Fund	20.00	303.65
3/4	567	CD Club	23.42	280.00
3/5		ATM withdrawal	40.00	250.00
3/11	568	Clothing	113.45	136.55
3/11		ATM withdrawal	40.00	96.55
3/15		Deposit	177.23	277.78
3/28	569	Car payment	100.00	177.78
3/28		ATM withdrawal	20.00	207.78
3/30		Deposit	184.16	391.94

Bank Ending Balance:	________	Adjusted Register Balance:	________
Add Outstanding Deposits:	________	Subtract Bank Charges:	________
Subtract Outstanding Checks:	________		________
Adjusted Bank Balance:	________	Reconciled Register Balance:	________

1. After balancing your register, how much money do you have in your account as of March 31?

____

____

2. What changes did you make?

____

____

Student Class Instructor

Date Assigned Date Completed

CHAPTER 5 Banking

Your Financial Portfolio Worksheet

Comparison Shopping for Banking Services

Compare banking services that are available to you. List the services that are important to you. Then call or visit several banks in your area and compare services, costs, and interest rates.

Name of Institution		
Address/phone number		
Savings		
Annual interest rate		
Minimum balance required		
Interest rate for:		
6-month CD		
1-year CD		
Money market account		
Checking		
Monthly service charge		
Minimum balance for "free" checking		
Fees for:		
ATM		
Printing checks		
Bouncing a check		
Stopping payment of check		
Copy of canceled check		
Return canceled checks		
Other		
Overdraft protection		

Student Class Instructor

Date Assigned Date Completed

Service		
Banking hours		
Location		
Number of ATMs		
24-hour phone service		
Other		

What services are most important to you?

Which bank would you choose? Explain why.

Student _______________ Class _______________ Instructor _______________

Date Assigned _______________ Date Completed _______________

CHAPTER 5 Banking

Finance Online: Researching CDs

Right now you probably have many dreams. Maybe you would like to start a business someday. Perhaps you hope to travel the world. The first step toward achieving your dreams will be making a plan to save money, which might include certificates of deposit. For this activity, you will research CDs on the Internet. Use an Internet search engine to find CDs and their rates. Once you have a list of specific CDs, choose one and answer the questions below.

Keywords Used	Site Name	Web Site Addresses	Information Offered

1. What is the interest rate for this CD if the term is one year? If the term is three years?

____

____

2. What is the minimum amount you could deposit?

____

Are there penalties for early withdrawals? What are they?

____

____

____

____

____

____

Student Class Instructor

Date Assigned Date Completed

CHAPTER 5 Banking

Software Activity (Optional)

Quicken Application

Using Quicken to Reconcile a Bank Account

OBJECTIVE: *To use a financial software application to track activity within a bank account and to reconcile the account records to the bank statement.*

Practice Situation

Juan Alvarez uses Quicken software to record his checking account activity. On October 31 he recorded the beginning balance in his checking account. Throughout the month of November, Juan recorded all checks written and deposits made. His bank statement for the month ended November 30 has arrived and contains the following information:

10/31	Beginning Statement Balance		$1,250.00
11/30	Ending Statement Balance		2,250.82
	Checks Paid	101	45.50
		102	59.68
		103	122.00
		104	450.00
		107	111.00
11/10	Deposits Cleared		1,800.00
11/15	Service Charge		11.00

Use Quicken to reconcile Juan's checking account, then print a register report for the account and answer the questions that follow.

Quicken Directions

1. Start your Quicken software and open problem **SA05.qdf.**
2. Click **Cash Flow** in the top Quicken menu bar.
3. Select the option *Reconcile.*
4. Select *Juan's Checking Account* to reconcile. Click **OK.**
5. Enter the statement ending balance in the Ending Balance field.
6. Enter the service charge amount in the Service Charge field.

7. Enter the Service Charge date by typing in or by clicking on the calendar icon. Click **OK.**
8. Mark each check that was paid by the bank by clicking in the **Clr** column to the left of each check detail.
9. Mark the deposits cleared by the bank by clicking in the **Clr** column to the left of each deposit.
10. In the bottom right corner of your screen, the **Difference** between the **Cleared Balance** and the **Statement Ending Balance** should be $0.00. If not, you may have missed an item or marked the wrong item. Correct any errors, then click *Finished.*
11. To save your work to a disk, click **File** in the Quicken menu. Select *File Operations,* then *Copy.* Label your new file **SA05***.qdf.** (Replace *** with your initials.) Type **A:** as the Location.
12. View the check register for Juan's checking account. Using the **Cash Flow** menu, select *Cash Flow Accounts.* Click *Juan's Checking Account.* Print the report if your teacher has requested that you do so.

Interpreting Results

1. What total cash outflows were recorded on Juan's checking account bank statement? ______________________

2. After reconciling Juan's checking account, which checks were outstanding (not paid) at 11/30? ______________________

3. What is the ending balance for Juan's checking account per his checking account register? ______________________

Drawing Conclusions

1. As you can see from the register report, Quicken assigns checks and deposits into categories. Explain the benefits to this method of organization.

____

____

____

2. Many individuals do not reconcile their bank accounts on a regular basis. Can you describe the benefits that you see of a regular bank account reconciliation?

____

____

____

____

Student Class Instructor

Date Assigned Date Completed

CHAPTER 5 Banking

SELF-ASSESSMENT QUIZ

DIRECTIONS: *Identify the letter of the choice that best completes the statement or answers the question.*

1. A possible drawback to using an ATM for your daily cash needs is (A) uncertainty about how much you will need (B) the service fee for its use (C) running up a large bill (D) interest charges.
2. The most commonly used payment service is a (A) savings account (B) certificate of deposit (C) checking account (D) mutual fund.
3. An automatic payment is when your (A) employer deposits your paycheck (B) bank withdraws money for a bill (C) friends use your PIN (D) local ATM accesses your account.
4. Using a debit card to pay for a meal at a restaurant is called (A) a point-of-sale transaction (B) a trade-off (C) a direct deposit (D) an online transaction.
5. Which financial institutions generally charge the highest interest rates on loans? (A) credit unions (B) mutual savings banks (C) commercial banks (D) finance companies
6. The interest rate varies from month to month on money in a (A) regular savings account (B) money market account (C) certificate of deposit (D) U.S. Savings Bond.
7. The rate of return on an investment is greatest when the interest is compounded (A) daily (B) weekly (C) monthly (D) yearly.
8. What is the annual percentage yield on a deposit of $200 in an account that pays 8% interest compounded twice a year ? (A) 4% (B) 8% (C) 8.16% (D) 16%
9. An activity account usually requires a (A) fee for each check (B) minimum balance (C) direct deposit of paychecks (D) certain balance in a savings account.
10. If a check is lost or stolen, you might ask the bank for (A) overdraft protection (B) copies of canceled checks (C) a stop-payment order (D) a bank reconciliation form.

Student ______ Class ______ Instructor ______

Date Assigned ______ Date Completed ______

CHAPTER 6 Consumer Credit

Reviewing Key Terms: Complete the Sentence

DIRECTIONS: *Using terms from the following list, complete the sentences below. Write the letter of the item you have chosen in the space provided.*

A. credit	D. line of credit	G. simple interest
B. consumer credit	E. finance charge	H. minimum monthly payment
C. closed-end credit	F. annual percentage rate	I. co-signing
		J. indebtedness

1. The total dollar amount a person pays to use credit is the ______.
2. The use of credit for personal needs is called ______.
3. ______ is computed only on the principal.
4. The condition of being deeply in debt is called ______.
5. The ______ is the cost of credit on a yearly basis, expressed as a percentage.
6. ______ a loan means agreeing to be responsible for loan payments if the borrower fails to make them.
7. A one-time loan that is paid back over a specified period of time and in payments of equal amounts is called ______.
8. An arrangement to receive cash, goods, or services now and pay for them in the future is called ______.
9. The maximum amount of money that a creditor makes available to a person is the ______.
10. The smallest amount a borrower can pay on a credit card bill and remain a borrower in good standing is the ______.

Student Class Instructor

Date Assigned Date Completed

CHAPTER 6 Consumer Credit

Understanding Key Concepts

DIRECTIONS: *On a separate sheet of paper, answer the questions below.*

1. Virginia is trying to decide whether to finance her purchase of a used Mustang convertible. What seven questions should Virginia ask herself before making her decision?
2. To finance a sofa for his new apartment, Calvin signed a contract to pay for the sofa in six equal installments. What type of consumer credit is Calvin using?
3. List the advantages and disadvantages of using credit.
4. Drew's monthly net income is $800. What is the maximum he should use on debt payments?
5. Aiku plans to spend $7,000 on video equipment. She is willing to spend some of her $10,000 in savings. However, she wants to finance the rest and pay it off in small monthly installments out of the $400 a month she earns working part-time. How might she obtain a low interest rate and make low monthly payments?
6. Janina has always paid cash for her purchases, including a Corvette and a truck she uses for her catering business. Now she wants to apply for a mortgage to buy a town home. For which one of the "five Cs of credit" does Janina qualify and for which one does she not qualify? What questions is a creditor likely to ask her to find out about the other "Cs"?
7. How might you prevent a thief from stealing personal credit information from your trash?
8. Which law allows a borrower to sue a creditor or credit bureau that verifies incorrect data about his or her credit history?
9. What does the Consumer Credit Counseling Service offer?
10. The DeWitts underestimated earnings from their family-owned business last year and neglected to make large enough quarterly income-tax payments. At tax time, they charged the $20,000 still owed to the government. Now the DeWitts owe a large credit card debt. Would you recommend that they apply for bankruptcy? Why or why not?

Student Class Instructor

Date Assigned Date Completed

CHAPTER 6 Consumer Credit

Activity 1: *Help a Friend Make a Decision*

SCANS COMPETENCIES ACHIEVED
Reading, Writing, Reasoning, Problem solving, Responsibility, Interpreting and communicating information

OBJECTIVE: *Determine the issues you need to think through before getting a credit card.*

You have just received an offer for a credit card. Based on what you learned in this chapter, make a list of four questions you need to ask yourself or the credit card company in order to make a wise decision. Write your questions in the left-hand column of the chart. In the right-hand column, explain why the question is important to ask.

Question	Why It's Important

Student ______ Class ______ Instructor ______

Date Assigned ______ Date Completed ______

CHAPTER 6 Consumer Credit

Activity 2: *Obtaining an Inexpensive Loan*

SCANS COMPETENCIES ACHIEVED

Writing, Creative thinking, Problem solving, Responsibility, Organizing and maintaining information

OBJECTIVE: *Think through the process of obtaining a loan.*

As you read in the chapter, many factors affect how much a loan will cost you. Some of these factors are listed below. For each factor, determine whether it would drive the overall cost of a loan up or down. Put those items which will make a loan more expensive on the "Up" arrow and those factors which would make a loan less expensive on the "Down" arrow.

borrowing from family members
borrowing from credit union
high APR
collateral
large down payment
shorter term
simple interest on declining balance
making minimum monthly payments
borrowing from retail stores
borrowing from finance companies
low APR
add-on interest
minimal down payment
longer term
simple interest

↑

______ ______
______ ______
______ ______
______ ______
______ ______
______ ______
______ ______
______ ______

↓

Student _______________ Class _______________ Instructor _______________

Date Assigned _______________ Date Completed _______________

Your friend Serena is a musician and wants to buy a baby grand piano. She has found one at a good price, $8,500, but she only has $42.66 in her savings account. She is thinking about taking out a loan and has come to you for advice. Drawing on what you have learned about the factors affecting the overall cost of a loan, list four different ways that Serena might obtain an inexpensive loan.

1. ______________________________

2. ______________________________

3. ______________________________

4. ______________________________

Student Class Instructor

Date Assigned Date Completed

CHAPTER 6 Consumer Credit

Math-Building Skills: Comparing Loan Applicants

DIRECTIONS: *Imagine you are a loan officer for a commercial bank. You are looking at two applications for consumer credit, a loan requiring a monthly repayment of $200. Below you'll find some financial information on the two applicants. Study the information. Then, using what you learned from the chapter, decide which applicant you consider the better loan risk. Explain the reasons for your answer, including a discussion of each person's debt payments-to-income ratio.*

Applicant A

monthly net income:	$1,350
car loan, monthly payment:	$200
rent:	$250
share of utilities:	$90
current savings:	$6,500

Applicant B

monthly net income:	$1,895
car loan, monthly payment:	$360
monthly payment on outstanding credit card balance:	$120
rent:	$410
share of utilities:	$130
current savings:	$2,400

Student | Class | Instructor

Date Assigned | Date Completed

CHAPTER 6 Consumer Credit

Your Financial Portfolio Worksheet

Credit Cards: Getting the Best Deal

Research two credit card companies. List their fees and any advantages they offer. Record your findings on the form below.

Credit card company		
Phone number		
Annual percentage rate (APR)		
Introductory rate		
Annual fee		
Grace period		
Cash advance fee		
Late payment fee		
Credit limit for new customers		
Premium offers and services:		
Travel accident insurance		
Protection if the card is lost or stolen		
Cash rebates on purchases		
Extensions on manufacturers' warranties		
Airline frequent flier miles		
Discounts on car rentals		
Can be linked to bank account		
Other gifts or incentives:		

Student Class Instructor

Date Assigned Date Completed

CHAPTER 6 Consumer Credit

If you wanted a credit card, which company would you prefer? Explain why.

Would you be influenced by the offer of airline miles or long-distance discounts? Why or why not?

Student Class Instructor

Date Assigned Date Completed

CHAPTER 6 Consumer Credit

Finance Online: Consumer Credit

The Consumer Credit Counseling Service is a lifesaver for many people in debt. Who else benefits from this nonprofit community service? Who pays for the services it offers?

For this activity, use an Internet search engine to find branches of the Consumer Credit Counseling Service across the country. Choose one in your area and one in another part of the country. Visit the Web sites to find out who funds the offices.

Keywords Used	Site Name	Web Site Addresses	Information Offered

1. What is the location of the Consumer Credit Counseling Service nearest you?

2. Where does this office get most of its funding?

3. Compare the services and funding sources in the offices at the different Web sites.

Student Class Instructor

Date Assigned Date Completed

CHAPTER 6 Consumer Credit

Software Activity (Optional)

Quicken Application

Calculating the Total Cost of a Financed Purchase

OBJECTIVE: *To determine the total cost of a financed purchase and to understand the impact of debt payments on personal net worth.*

Practice Situation

Ralph purchased a stereo system from Circuit City. The store offered him a credit account to make the purchase, at an interest rate of 16.9 percent, compounding monthly. Ralph has agreed to pay the total amount due in one year. The stereo cost including tax and warranty is $3,546.35. Assume Ralph makes the purchase on January 1. Ralph's monthly net income is $3,500. Ralph wants to use Quicken to track his payments to Circuit City. He has already set up the loan to Circuit City and has recorded his new asset, labeled "Stereo System" in Quicken. Review the loan summary in the software application, print the payment schedule, and answer the questions that follow. Compute his debt-payments-to-income ratio.

Quicken Directions

1. Start your Quicken software program and open the data file **SA06.qdf.**
2. Click on the side navigation tab, **Property & Debt Center.** As you can see, the *Property and Debt Accounts* contain Ralph's "Stereo System" and "Circuit City" accounts.
3. Review the *Loan Accounts Summary* information below *Property & Debt Accounts*. Verify that the terms of the credit agreement are properly reflected.
4. Click on the **Make a Payment** button. Click the **Payment Schedule** tab.
5. Print Ralph's Payment Schedule by clicking on **Print** in the top menu bar of the View Loans window. You will use this schedule to answer the questions that follow.
6. Close your Quicken software program.

Interpreting Results

1. In order to pay off the total amount for Ralph's stereo system, what monthly payments are necessary? ____________

2. If Ralph adheres to his payment plan, how much total interest will he pay on the stereo purchase? ____________

3. What amount will Ralph's final payment be on the stereo? In which month will this final payment occur?

____

4. Assuming that Ralph has made only one credit purchase, what is Ralph's debt-payments-to-income ratio?

____

Drawing Conclusions

1. What total amount, including interest, did Ralph pay for his stereo system?

____

2. Is Ralph's debt-payment-to-income ratio within the recommended range? Explain.

____

____

____

Student ______ **Class** ______ **Instructor** ______

Date Assigned ______ **Date Completed** ______

CHAPTER 6 Consumer Credit

SELF-ASSESSMENT QUIZ

DIRECTIONS: *Circle the letter of the choice that best completes the statement or answers the question.*

1. The periodic charge for using credit is called (A) financing (B) interest (C) installment payments (D) a credit limit.
2. The greatest disadvantage of using credit cards is (A) having a record of expenses (B) being in physical danger (C) proving to be a responsible spender (D) being tempted to overspend.
3. You will probably find the least expensive loan from (A) a commercial bank (B) a finance company (C) family members (D) a home equity loan.
4. The usual trade-off of choosing small payments is (A) having a short period to pay (B) paying more in interest (C) having variable interest rates (D) pledging collateral.
5. No matter how often you make payments, interest is calculated on the full amount of the original principal with the (A) simple interest method (B) declining balance method (C) add-on interest method (D) up-front cash method.
6. Which of the "five Cs of credit" does your income affect? (A) capacity (B) character (C) collateral (D) credit history
7. Which law gives a borrower the right to stop payment? (A) Equal Credit Opportunity Act (B) Fair Credit Reporting Act (C) Fair Credit Billing Act (D) Truth in Lending Act
8. Under the Equal Credit Opportunity Act, you may sue a creditor if the creditor (A) discriminates against you (B) fails to disclose information (C) gives inaccurate information (D) hires a collection agency.
9. The legal process in which some or all of a debtor's assets are distributed among creditors because the debtor cannot pay his or her debts is called (A) debt collection (B) credit counseling (C) adjusted repayment (D) bankruptcy.
10. Chapter 7 bankruptcy relieves an individual from debts arising from (A) alimony (B) credit card charges (C) child support (D) fraud.

Student ______________________ Class ______________ Instructor ______________

Date Assigned ______________________ Date Completed ______________________

CHAPTER 7 The Finances of Housing

Reviewing Key Terms: Complete the Sentence

DIRECTIONS: *Using terms from the following list, complete the sentences below. Write the letter of the term you have chosen in the space provided.*

A. mobility	D. equity	G. adjustable-rate mortgage
B. lease	E. escrow account	H. refinance
C. security deposit	F. points	I. title insurance
		J. appraisal

1. ______ is the value of a home less the amount still owed on the money borrowed to purchase it.

2. A(n) ______ has an interest rate that increases or decreases during the life of the loan.

3. ______ is an estimate of the current value of a property.

4. The ability to move easily from place to place is called ______.

5. Money in a(n) ______ is held in trust until it can be delivered to the designated party.

6. An amount of money paid to the owner of a property by a tenant to guard against any financial loss that the tenant might cause is called a(n) ______.

7. An extra interest charge that a home buyer must pay in order to get a lower interest rate on a mortgage is called ______.

8. ______ protects the home buyer in case problems with the title are found in the future.

9. A(n) ______ is a legal document that defines the conditions of a rental agreement between a tenant and a landlord.

10. When homeowners ______, they take out a new mortgage at a lower interest rate.

Student Class Instructor

Date Assigned Date Completed

CHAPTER 7 The Finances of Housing

Understanding Key Concepts

DIRECTIONS: *On a separate sheet of paper, answer the questions below.*

1. Noemi is an apprentice carpenter who would like to live the rest of her life in the neighborhood where she grew up. She plans to host frequent parties for her many family members and friends but cannot afford the large, elegant houses in the real estate agent's listings. What kind of housing would you recommend for Noemi? Explain your answer.
2. Martin is an actor who travels to different locations to perform in plays and in movies. He spends much of his time auditioning; learning scripts; and networking with directors, agents, and other actors. Sometimes the run of his play is cut short, and he scrapes by without a paycheck for weeks. Is Martin more likely to rent or buy a home? Explain your answer.
3. How does a lease usually protect the tenant in most states?
4. Catherine and Jim have finally paid off their home mortgage. What house-related financial obligations do they still have?
5. List three factors that will help working parents Claudia and Steve decide where to buy a house.
6. When might a buyer consider offering more than the listing price for a house?
7. What serves as collateral when a home buyer takes out a mortgage loan, and what happens if he or she fails to repay the loan?
8. Mary has paid two years on a 20-year mortgage at 8% interest. Since taking out the loan, she received a raise and would like to pay off her loan more quickly. Mary has found a bank that will refinance her mortgage for 15 years at the same rate of 8% interest plus $2,000 in fees. What would you advise Mary to do? Why?
9. Who qualifies for home loans from the Federal Housing Administration?
10. Name three typical closing costs.

Student _______________ Class _______________ Instructor _______________

Date Assigned _______________ Date Completed _______________

CHAPTER 7 The Finances of Housing

Activity 1: *Examine a Rental Lease*

SCANS COMPETENCIES ACHIEVED

Reading, Writing, Reasoning, Problem solving, Acquiring and evaluating information, Self-management

OBJECTIVE: *Obtain and evaluate a rental lease.*

In this activity, you'll examine a lease to get a sense of what they typically include. This knowledge will make you better prepared when your new landlord hands you one to sign. Obtain a rental lease from an apartment complex rental office near you, from a housing agency, or from someone you know who is a landlord. Then answer the following questions.

1. How long does the lease run?

____

2. How much is the rent and on what day of the month is it due?

____

3. How much notice do you need to give before you move out?

____

4. Who pays for water, heat, electricity, and other utilities?

____

5. Can you have pets? If so, how many and what kinds?

____

6. Is there a restriction on how many people can live in the apartment? If so, what is the limit?

____

7. Can you make changes to the apartment? If so, what kinds?

____

8. Are there any restrictions on your activities, such as playing your stereo? Describe them.

____

9. What is the procedure for settling disputes with the landlord?

____

10. After evaluating the lease, would you rent this apartment? Why or why not?

____

Student Class Instructor

Date Assigned Date Completed

CHAPTER 7 The Finances of Housing

Activity 2: *Comparing Housing Options*

SCANS COMPETENCIES ACHIEVED

Reading, Writing, Teaching others, Problem solving, Decision making, Reasoning, Seeing things in the mind's eye

OBJECTIVE: *Determine which kind of housing is best for you by assessing your attitudes.*

Some people like houses in the suburbs for the sense of stability they offer, while others prefer the flexibility of an apartment in the city. Some want to own; others want the freedom of renting. In this activity you'll use a scale to determine your housing preferences.

On the next page, you'll find some statements. For each statement, circle the number on the scale that corresponds to the way you feel about it. Then, exchange completed exercises, including this page, with a partner. Read his or her rankings on the scales. Then write a recommendation in the space below about what kind of housing seems most suitable for your partner.

Student	Class	Instructor
Date Assigned	Date Completed	

Circle the number that best matches how you feel about the statement.

1. I want the security that comes from owning my own home.

5 Strongly agree	4	3	2	1 Strongly disagree

2. The freedom to easily change my living situation is important.

5 Strongly agree	4	3	2	1 Strongly disagree

3. I want to live near movies, clubs, and other types of entertainment.

5 Strongly agree	4	3	2	1 Strongly disagree

4. Living around a lot of other people like me would be a lot of fun.

5 Strongly agree	4	3	2	1 Strongly disagree

5. The type of home that I grew up in will always be the ideal for me.

5 Strongly agree	4	3	2	1 Strongly disagree

6. It would be hard for me to live without pets.

5 Strongly agree	4	3	2	1 Strongly disagree

7. I need to put my own stamp on any place I live.

5 Strongly agree	4	3	2	1 Strongly disagree

8. Yard work and home maintenance chores are my idea of drudgery.

5 Strongly agree	4	3	2	1 Strongly disagree

9. It would be nice to live near work so I wouldn't have to commute a long distance.

5 Strongly agree	4	3	2	1 Strongly disagree

10. The idea of taking on a mortgage frightens me.

5 Strongly agree	4	3	2	1 Strongly disagree

Student ______ Class ______ Instructor ______

Date Assigned ______ Date Completed ______

CHAPTER 7 The Finances of Housing

Math-Building Skills: Nate and Lindsay Buy a House

Choosing the best mortgage would be easy, if all you had to do was look at the interest rate. Of course, with points, closing costs, and other charges, you have to make sure you're comparing apples to apples. The only way to find out the real cost of each mortgage package is to do the math.

DIRECTIONS: *Read the scenario. Then answer the questions below.*

Nate and Lindsay have found a house they like in a neighborhood they want to live in. The price of the house is $120,000. They plan to make a down payment of $24,000 or 20%. They have received quotes for 30-year fixed mortgages from three lenders:

- **Washington Federal** offered a rate of 8.38% with 1.25 points and additional closing costs to the buyer of $2,000.
- **Adams National Bank** offered a rate of 8.63% with no points and additional closing costs to the buyer of $3,300.
- **Jefferson Savings** offered a rate of 8.5% with 1 point and additional closing costs to the buyer of $2,500.

1. How much money will Nate and Lindsay need to borrow? ______

2. How much will Nate and Lindsay pay at closing with each loan package?

a. Washington Federal ______

b. Adams National Bank ______

c. Jefferson Savings ______

3. Which package will give them the lowest monthly payment?

______

4. Based on your answers, which mortgage loan would you recommend they choose? Why?

______

______

______

______

______

______

______

Student _______________ Class _______________ Instructor _______________

Date Assigned _______________ Date Completed _______________

CHAPTER 7 The Finances of Housing

Your Financial Portfolio Worksheet

Renting Versus Buying Your Place of Residence

Check a newspaper for a typical rental price for a two-bedroom apartment and a typical selling price for a two-bedroom house. Use those figures to complete your comparison. How do your figures compare?

Rental Costs	
Annual rent payments (monthly rent $_____ × 12)	
Renter's insurance	250
Total annual cost of renting	

Buying Costs	
Down payment (10%) **Purchase price ×.10 = down payment**	
Annual mortgage payment (use interest factor 0.0878) **Purchase price − down payment = loan amount** **Loan amount × 0.0878 = annual mortgage payment**	
Annual property taxes (1.5% of purchase price)	
Annual mortgage insurance premium (.007 × loan amount)	
Homeowner's insurance (annual premium)	400
Estimated annual maintenance and repairs (1% of purchase price)	

Student Class Instructor

Date Assigned Date Completed

Financial benefits of home ownership:	
Less: Tax savings for mortgage interest (estimate)	−2,866
Less: Tax savings for property taxes (annual property taxes times 27% tax rate)	
Total cost of buying first year	
Less: One-time down payment (from above)	
Less: Estimated annual appreciation (average 4% increase on the purchase price)	
Total long-term annual cost of buying	

Using the figures in your comparison, will it be less expensive the first year to rent or buy? In the long term, will it be less expensive to rent or buy?

Student _______________ Class _______________ Instructor _______________

Date Assigned _______________ Date Completed _______________

CHAPTER 7 The Finances of Housing

Finance Online: The Finances of Housing

What kind of house would you like to buy someday? How many rooms will it have? Do you want a patio? A garden? An attached garage? What will a house like this cost you each month in mortgage payments?

For this activity, use an Internet search engine to find out about available houses. Choose the house closest to your ideal. Note the house's listing price. Then check the Internet for available interest rates on 30-year conventional mortgages. Next, find an amortization table or loan calculator to help you determine the size of monthly mortgage payments at different rates.

Keywords Used	Site Name	Web Site Addresses	Information Offered

1. Describe your choice of house. What was the price listed for this house?

____

____

2. Imagine you can make a 10% down payment on the house. What would be the amount of your mortgage loan? What interest rate did you find for a 30-year mortgage?

____

____

3. At the lowest available interest rate, what would be the monthly payment on your mortgage loan?

____

____

Student | Class | Instructor

Date Assigned | Date Completed

CHAPTER 7 The Finances of Housing

Software Activity (Optional)

Spreadsheet Application

Comparing Housing Alternatives

OBJECTIVE: *To effectively compare and analyze the financial implications involved in a buy-versus-rent decision.*

Practice Situation

The following data represents two housing alternatives. Alternative 1 presents the costs associated with renting an apartment. Alternative 2 offers data related to the purchase of a home. Calculate the annual total expenses required for each option, then answer the questions that follow.

Alternative 1: An apartment is available at a monthly rent of $750. Renters insurance will cost $75 per quarter. A $1000 security deposit is required on the apartment.

Alternative 2: The cost of a home is $95,000. You are considering a 30-year conventional fixed-rate mortgage. The mortgage interest rate is 8 percent and you plan to pay a down payment of $9,500. The monthly payment will be $627. You will pay approximately $6,800 in mortgage interest for the first year. You anticipate that closing costs will be $2,000. The annual property taxes are estimated to be $2,500, and homeowners insurance has been computed to be $500. You anticipate spending approximately 1.5 percent of the cost of the home per year for its maintenance. Assume that homes in your geographic area appreciate at approximately 3 percent of their cost annually.

For both alternatives, assume an after-tax savings interest rate of 5 percent and a tax rate of 30 percent.

Spreadsheet Directions

1. Start your spreadsheet software program and open problem **SA07.xls.** Use the information presented for each alternative and enter the data into the spreadsheet. Remember to use formulas to calculate annual amounts.
2. Format all dollar amounts to Currency, 2 decimals.
3. Insert the formulas to compute tax savings for mortgage interest and property taxes by multiplying the payments by the tax rate.
4. Insert the formulas to compute the Total Annual Cost of Renting and the Total Annual Cost of Buying.

5. Perform your calculations and complete the spreadsheet, then save your work to a new file labeled **SA07***.xls.** (Replace *** with your initials.)
6. Print out a copy of your work if your teacher has instructed you to do so.

Interpreting Results

1. What is the total annual cost associated with each housing alternative?

____

2. Based on your calculations for alternative 2, what actual total cash outlay would be required in the first year of the purchase?

____

____

____

Drawing Conclusions

1. Based upon your computations, which scenario would be the favorable decision based on financial considerations? Explain.

____

____

2. What other nonfinancial advantages and disadvantages should be considered for each alternative?

____

____

____

____

Student Class Instructor

Date Assigned Date Completed

CHAPTER 7 The Finances of Housing

SELF-ASSESSMENT QUIZ

DIRECTIONS: *Circle the letter of the choice that best completes the statement or answers the question.*

1. An advantage of owning a house instead of renting is that you (A) do maintenance yourself (B) can move easily (C) may have tax advantages (D) need less money.
2. If a tenant fails to pay rent or damages the property, the lease gives the landlord the right to (A) increase the rent (B) take legal action (C) throw the tenant out (D) lock out the tenant.
3. The most popular type of housing in the United States is (A) single-family dwellings (B) multiunit dwellings (C) condominiums (D) mobile homes.
4. A real estate agent provides all the following services EXCEPT (A) supplying locations of available houses (B) evaluating a house's soundness (C) negotiating a purchase price (D) recommending lawyers and insurance agents.
5. Owners might accept less than they think their house is worth when (A) homes are in high demand (B) the house fits the buyer's ideal of a home (C) the interest rates are low (D) they need to move in a hurry.
6. The portion of the purchase price that a buyer pays the seller when signing a purchase agreement is called the (A) earnest money (B) escrow (C) application fee (D) down payment.
7. Generally mortgage insurance is required when the buyer's down payment is (A) 10% (B) 20% (C) 25% (D) 30%.
8. In the first years of a mortgage, most of the monthly payment goes toward paying off the (A) points (B) property taxes (C) principal (D) interest.
9. What might a homeowner do to get a lower interest rate? (A) default (B) take a second mortgage (C) refinance (D) amortize.
10. An example of a closing cost is the fee for (A) garbage removal (B) title insurance (C) homeowner's insurance (D) an appraisal.

Student Class Instructor

Date Assigned Date Completed

CHAPTER 8 The Fundamentals of Investing

Reviewing Key Terms: Complete the Sentence

DIRECTIONS: *Using terms from the following list, complete the sentences below. Write the letter of the term you have chosen in the space provided.*

A. speculative investment	D. common stock	G. mutual fund
B. retained earnings	E. preferred stock	H. diversification
C. equity capital	F. corporate bond	I. capital gain
		J. annual report

1. Money that a business gets from its owners in order to operate is ______.
2. ______ gives the owner the advantage of receiving cash dividends before common stockholders receive any.
3. The process of spreading assets among several different types of investments to lessen risk is called ______.
4. A corporation's written pledge to repay a specified amount of money along with interest to an investor is called a ______.
5. All publicly owned corporations send investors a(n) ______.
6. The profit from the sale of an asset such as stocks, bonds, or real estate is a ______.
7. A high-risk stock bought in the hope of earning a relatively large profit in a short time is called a(n) ______.
8. Profits that are reinvested in the company are called ______.
9. The most basic form of corporate ownership is ______, and it entitles the owner to voting privileges in the company.
10. An investment alternative in which investors pool their money to buy stocks, bonds, and other securities based on selections by professional managers who work for an investment company is called a(n) ______.

Student Class Instructor

Date Assigned Date Completed

CHAPTER 8 The Fundamentals of Investing

Understanding Key Concepts

DIRECTIONS: *On a separate sheet of paper, answer the questions below.*

1. Describe which savings method you plan to use when you begin working full time.
2. Which would you prefer to make: a safe investment or a speculative one? Explain your choice.
3. Michiko's parents purchased a government bond for $10,000 at 5% interest for their daughter. When rates on government bonds rose to 8%, Michiko sold the bond before its maturity date. How much did she lose? Which component of risk caused her loss?
4. Angel wants to buy a house in five or six years. He plans to obtain the down payment by investing in stock now and then selling it when he finds the right house. Would you recommend that he buy stock in a "growth" company? Why or why not?
5. Explain three ways that common stock can show growth potential for the stockholder.
6. Why is a mutual fund often a safe way to invest?
7. Put the following steps of developing a personal investment plan in the correct order: (a) Determine the amount of money you have to invest. (b) Establish investment goals. (c) Recheck your investment program periodically. (d) List all the investments you want to evaluate. (e) Decide how much money you will need in order to reach your goals by a particular date. (f) Reduce the list of possible investments to a reasonable number. (g) Choose at least two investments to give yourself some diversity. (h) Evaluate the risk and potential return for all the investments on your list.
8. Give three examples of investments that earn tax-deferred income.
9. Marie Claire, a geologist, often works for several weeks collecting rock samples in remote areas. She has no access to television, newspapers, or business periodicals but wonders how her stocks are doing. What other sources of information might she use?
10. How do services provided by Standard and Poor's Stock Reports and Morningstar Investment Reports differ?

Student Class Instructor

Date Assigned Date Completed

CHAPTER 8 The Fundamentals of Investing

Activity 1: *A Friend in Need*

SCANS COMPETENCIES ACHIEVED

Writing, Reasoning, Problem solving, Interpreting and communicating information, Teaching others

OBJECTIVE: *Give advice to a friend who wants to start an investment program.*

A friend of yours knows you're taking a business and personal finance class and has heard you talk about how much you're learning. She asks you for some advice on how to get her financial house in order; specifically, she wants to attend the local technical college to study to become an emergency medical technician (EMT). Using what you learned in this chapter, write a letter to your friend, giving her sound advice on how to begin investing her money to attain her goal. Use the space below for your letter. Use a separate sheet of paper to prewrite, make notes, and organize your thoughts, or if your letter is too long to fit in the space below.

Student | Class | Instructor

Date Assigned | Date Completed

CHAPTER 8 The Fundamentals of Investing

Activity 2: *Researching Investments*

SCANS COMPETENCIES ACHIEVED

Reading, Writing, Creative Thinking, Decision making, Problem solving, Knowing how to learn, Acquiring and evaluating information, Organizing and maintaining information, Allocating money

OBJECTIVE: *Decide how to invest a surprise $5,000 inheritance.*

Imagine that you have inherited $5,000 from your favorite great aunt. She included a letter in her will encouraging you to invest the money responsibly so that you can take advantage of the compounding effects of investing. This activity will let you practice allocating your investment funds in a responsible and informed way.

Using the Internet, personal finance magazines such as *Money, Consumer Reports, Smart Money, Kiplinger's Personal Finance,* and any other source of information you choose, create an investment plan. In your plan, you should list the following kinds of information: how much of the money you will place in which investment, how you learned about the investment, and what rate of return you expect to receive on the investment. Use the chart below to list your investment choices. A sample entry has been done for you. Then prepare a written evaluation of the investment choices.

	Investment				
	1	2	3	4	5
Name of Investment	Vanguard S&P 500 Stock Index Fund				
Type of Investment	Stock Mutual Fund				
Amount to Invest	$2,500				
Information Source	*Money* magazine				

Student Class Instructor

Date Assigned Date Completed

CHAPTER 8 The Fundamentals of Investing

Math-Building Skills: Examining Investment Performance

Comparing the performance over several years of different mutual fund investments can help you decide where to invest your money. In this activity, you'll use your math skills to examine the performances of some mutual funds.

DIRECTIONS: *The information below shows by what percentage your money would have grown if you had started investing in each of the following stock mutual funds on January 1, 2000. The data show the percentage of growth from January 1 to the next January 1. Using this information and a sheet of graph paper, create a line graph that shows the value and relative growth of an initial $1,000 investment in each of the three mutual funds.*

Madison Investment Trust: *January 1, 2001 (41%); January 1, 2002 (8%); January 1, 2003 (40%); January 1, 2004 (23%)*

Monroe Equity Fund: *January 1, 2001 (29%); January 1, 2002 (16%); January 1, 2003 (3%); January 1, 2004 (19%)*

Quincy Adams Fund: *January 1, 2001 (2%); January 1, 2002 (10%); January 1, 2003 (22%); January 1, 2004 (88%)*

Student	Class	Instructor
Date Assigned	Date Completed	

CHAPTER 8 The Fundamentals of Investing

Your Financial Portfolio Worksheet

Avoiding Future Shock

Choose a short- or long-term financial goal you would like to reach and use these guidelines to prepare an investment goal for yourself. Research some of the available investments and come up with your own investment alternatives.

Establish your goal:	
Amount of money needed:	
Initial amount to invest:	
Possible investment alternatives:	
Risk factor for each alternative:	
Projected return for each alternative:	
Top 3 choices:	
Final choice:	

Then in the space below explain your reasons for your final choice.

Student Class Instructor

Date Assigned Date Completed

CHAPTER 8 The Fundamentals of Investing

Finance Online: Preparing for an Investment Program

The Internet has a wealth of information about investments, but how do you find the facts you need?

Many people want to invest but do not have the time to follow the market. That is why mutual funds are popular; a professional manager monitors the market and makes the decisions for the investors. For this activity, use an Internet search engine to answer the following questions.

Keywords Used	Site Name	Web Site Addresses	Information Offered

1. Find the name of an investment firm. What services does it offer?

2. Name five mutual funds.

3. For what purposes other than retirement might an investor use an IRA?

Student _______________ Class _______________ Instructor _______________

Date Assigned _______________ Date Completed _______________

CHAPTER 8 The Fundamentals of Investing

Software Activity (Optional)

Spreadsheet Application

Charting the Performance of an Investment

OBJECTIVE: *To chart the performance of a stock price and calculate the total return on a stock transaction.*

Practice Situation

The following information illustrates the monthly price for a share of Eastman Kodak common stock.

January 1	$56	July 1	$55
February 1	$58	August 1	$56
March 1	$52	September 1	$59
April 1	$52	October 1	$61
May 1	$53	November 1	$62
June 1	$56	December 1	$63

Rachael Campbell purchased 300 shares of Eastman Kodak common stock on March 1. She paid a commission of $80. On December 1, Rachael sold all 300 shares. That commission was $85. Dividends were $3.36 per share for the period of March 1–December 1.

Use a spreadsheet to chart the price of one share of Eastman Kodak stock from January 1 through December 1. Next, compute the total return on Rachael's investment. Answer the questions that follow.

Spreadsheet Directions

1. Start your spreadsheet software program and open problem **SA08.xls.** Enter the monthly stock price data into the spreadsheet.
2. To create a chart of the stock price data you have entered, select **Insert** from the Toolbar at the top of the screen. Then, select **Chart** from the menu choices.
3. Choose *Column* as the type of chart you wish to create. Click *Next.*
4. Select the Data Range by clicking on the small spreadsheet icon to the right of the Data Range field. Then, on the spreadsheet, select the cells that contain the data and labels you want displayed in the chart. Click *Next.*
5. Type **Eastman Kodak Stock Prices** as the Chart title.
6. Type **Month** as the Category (X) axis. Type **Price** as the Value (Y) axis. Click *Next.*
7. For placement of the chart, select the option: *Set chart as object in Sheet 1.* Click *Finish.*
8. Your chart should now be inserted on the same spreadsheet as your data. You may click on the chart's edges to resize or drag it to another location within the sheet.
9. Enter the data for Rachael's stock transactions. First, enter the data for the purchase of the stock on March 1. Next, enter the data for the sale of the stock on December 1.
10. Compute the transaction summary information.

11. When your calculations are completed, save your work to a new file labeled **SA08***.xls.** (Replace *** with your initials.)
12. Print out a copy of your work if your teacher has instructed you to do so.

Interpreting Results

1. Based on the chart that you created for the stock prices of Eastman Kodak common stock, what is the overall trend of this investment? Explain.

____

____

2. What was Rachael's total return on her stock transactions at December 1?

____

Drawing Conclusions

1. In addition to the profit from the sale of the stock that Rachael gained, what other financial benefit did she experience from the Eastman Kodak stock transaction? Explain.

____

____

2. Discuss the financial implications involved when deciding to sell a stock investment. For example, if Rachael had sold her stock on November 1 instead of December 1, what implications would have been involved? Did Rachael choose a favorable time to sell her stock? Explain.

____

____

____

Student Class Instructor

Date Assigned Date Completed

CHAPTER 8 The Fundamentals of Investing

SELF-ASSESSMENT QUIZ

DIRECTIONS: *Circle the letter of the choice that best completes the statement or answers the question.*

1. A person risks losing most or all of his or her money in (A) a savings account (B) an elective savings program (C) a speculative investment (D) a conservative investment.
2. If a person loses buying power because he or she invests money at a fixed interest rate, the risk factor at fault is (A) inflation (B) business failure (C) interest rates (D) the market.
3. The formula for finding the value of a corporate bond if interest rates change is (A) Original Price × Loss of Buying Power (B) Market Price ÷ Annual Interest Earned (C) Annual Interest Earned ÷ New Interest Rate (D) New Interest Rate − Old Interest Rate.
4. Which investment is the safest source of income? (A) U.S. Treasury bills (B) corporate bonds (C) precious metals (D) collectibles
5. Stock in a company provides the stockholder with regular income when the company (A) reinvests its earnings (B) pays dividends (C) splits its stock (D) pays interest until maturity.
6. A major goal when investing in real estate is to (A) earn interest (B) receive dividends (C) have liquid assets (D) sell at a profit.
7. Which investment would most likely top an investment program "pyramid"? (A) U.S. Treasury bills (B) stock in a foreign company (C) mutual funds (D) certificates of deposit.
8. The federal government requires that the Securities and Exchange Commission (A) give exams to financial planners (B) issue licenses to planning companies (C) certify or charter financial planners (D) monitor large financial planning companies.
9. An example of an investment that produces tax-exempt income is (A) corporate bonds (B) IRAs (C) municipal bonds (D) 403(b) retirement plans.
10. The federal government requires that any corporation selling new issues of securities must provide investors with (A) the Survey of Current Business (B) a prospectus (C) a financial planner (D) an investors' service.

Student _______________ Class _______________ Instructor _______________

Date Assigned _______________ Date Completed _______________

CHAPTER 9 Stocks

Reviewing Key Terms: Complete the Sentence

DIRECTIONS: *Using terms from the following list, complete the sentences below. Write the letter of the term you have chosen in the space provided.*

A. securities	D. blue-chip stock	G. bull market
B. proxy	E. cyclical stock	H. bear market
C. par value	F. penny stock	I. round lot
		J. odd lot

1. Stock that is considered a conservative, safe investment is called ______.

2. A(n) ______ occurs when investors are pessimistic about the economy and sell stocks.

3. The assigned dollar amount that is printed on a stock certificate is the ______.

4. Stock that has a market value that reflects the state of the economy is called ______.

5. A(n) ______ contains fewer than 100 shares of a stock.

6. Investments such as stocks, bonds, mutual finds, options, and commodities are called ______.

7. A(n) ______ occurs when investors are optimistic about the economy and buy stocks.

8. A legal document that transfers a stockholder's voting rights to someone else is a(n) ______.

9. On the floors of the exchanges, stocks are traded in ______, or multiples of 100 shares of a particular stock.

10. New companies or companies whose sales are unsteady issue ______, which typically sell for less than $1 a share.

Student Class Instructor

Date Assigned Date Completed

CHAPTER 9 Stocks

Understanding Key Concepts

DIRECTIONS: *On a separate sheet of paper, answer the questions below.*

1. How does a preemptive right keep ownership of a corporation stable?
2. Explain the three ways investors can make money from common stock.
3. Compare the advantages and disadvantages of preferred stock and common stock.
4. Carmen wants to invest in a corporation whose potential earnings may be higher than the average earnings predicted for other companies. In other words, she wants a growth stock. What characteristics should Carmen look for in a corporation?
5. What is the difference between a large cap stock and a small cap stock?
6. Kelvin Company has 1,000,000 outstanding shares of common stock and net earnings of $650,000. What are Kelvin Company's earnings per share?
7. How do many companies use initial public offerings (IPOs)? Would you invest in IPOs? Explain your answer.
8. Bonnie wants to sell her shares in a fairly small software company and use her proceeds to buy Microsoft stock. In which marketplace will she conduct her transactions? Why?
9. Danny has an account with a brokerage firm, and his account executive does a lot of buying and selling of stocks in Danny's portfolio. The value of Danny's stocks has remained relatively constant yet he pays a lot in commissions. What is going on with Danny's account and what would you advise him to do?
10. Mai received $10,000 in gifts for her graduation from high school and wants to begin investing in the stock market. Which investment strategy would you recommend? Why?

Student ______________________ Class ______________ Instructor ______________

Date Assigned ______________________ Date Completed ______________________

CHAPTER 9 Stocks

Activity 1: *Factors Affecting Stock Prices*

> **SCANS COMPETENCIES ACHIEVED**
> Reading, Writing, Acquiring and evaluating information, Organizing and maintaining information

OBJECTIVE: *Examine what causes stock prices to rise or fall.*

You learned in this chapter about the factors that influence a stock's price to go up or down. Use the space provided to list these factors. Write the factors that cause a stock's price to rise on the arrows pointing up. Write the factors that pressure a stock's price to fall on the arrows pointing down.

Financial Web sites and stock advisory services like Value Line, Standard & Poor's, Moody's Investors Service, and Mergent Financial Investors Service (available at your community library) contain historical information about the stock prices. Choose a stock that interests you and find information about it in one of these resources.

1. Which stock did you choose?

____

2. Is the price rising or falling?

____

3. Which of the factors you listed seem to be responsible for the changes in price?

____

Student ______ Class ______ Instructor ______

Date Assigned ______ Date Completed ______

CHAPTER 9 Stocks

Activity 2: *Evaluating Stocks*

SCANS COMPETENCIES ACHIEVED

Reading, Math, Problem solving, Decision making, Acquiring and evaluating information, Organizing and maintaining information, Interpreting and communicating information

OBJECTIVE: *Evaluate various stocks for their investment potential.*

Obtaining and evaluating information is a key to making wise stock investments. In this activity, you'll assemble financial information on some well-known companies, organize it, and use it to evaluate investments.

On the next page, you'll find a chart with space for information about the stocks of several well-known companies. Use the financial section of a major newspaper or the Internet to find the information. Then answer the following questions.

1. Which stocks have the three highest PE ratios? ______

The three lowest? ______

2. Which three stocks are trading at nearest their 52-week highs? ______

Their 52-week lows? ______

3. Which three stocks pay the highest yield? ______

The lowest yield? ______

4. Which stock do you feel would be the best investment? Why?

______

______

______

5. Which stock do you feel would be the worst investment? Why?

______

______

______

Student Class Instructor

Date Assigned Date Completed

	Ticker Symbol	Current Price	52-week High	52-week Low	PE Ratio	Yield
Intel						
Microsoft						
Ford						
General Electric						
Coca-Cola						
Wal-Mart						
Amazon.com						
Chevron-Texaco						
Wells Fargo						
Disney						

Student ______ Class ______ Instructor ______

Date Assigned ______ Date Completed ______

CHAPTER 9 Stocks

Math-Building Skills: Dollar-Cost Averaging

DIRECTIONS: *Martin has been buying shares of PlantMania, a garden center chain, using dollar-cost averaging. He buys $100 worth of stock each purchase. Below are the prices of a share of the stock on the dates he made his purchases. How many shares did he buy on each date? Assume that he is able to buy fractions of shares and that he pays no commission for his purchases.*

Date	Price of a Share	Number of Shares Purchased
5/1/05	$12.50	______
8/12/05	$12.10	______
1/6/06	$13.25	______
4/16/06	$13.87	______
8/22/06	$14.92	______
2/16/07	$14.25	______
7/7/07	$15.68	______
12/28/07	$16.22	______
4/8/08	$16.92	______

For the following questions, assume the stock does not pay a dividend.

1. What is the total number of shares he now owns? ______
2. What is the average overall per-share price of his stock? ______
3. What is the value of his investment on the last purchase date? ______
4. What is the percentage total return? ______

Student Class Instructor

Date Assigned Date Completed

CHAPTER 9 Stocks

Your Financial Portfolio Worksheet

Investing in Stock

Choose a stock you would like to invest in and research it. You can get stock information about a company in the financial section of major newspapers, the Internet, and from the companies themselves. You can also find information from *Standard & Poor's Stock and Bond Guide, Handbook of Common Stocks,* or *Value Line Investment Survey.*

Take Stock of Your Future	
Company name and address	
What types of product(s) or service(s) does the company provide?	
What was the highest price paid per share during the past 52 weeks?	
What was the lowest price paid per share in the past 52 weeks?	
What is the current price paid per share?	
What is the price-earnings (PE) ratio?	
What are the company's earnings per share for the last three years?	
Is the company currently paying dividends? If so, how much?	
Have profits increased over the last seven years?	
List any additional information from a stock advisory service, such as *Standard & Poor's Stock and Bond Guide.*	

Student Class Instructor

Date Assigned Date Completed

What type of stock would you be interested in purchasing? Explain why.

Do you think the company you chose to research would be a wise investment choice? Explain your answer.

Student | Class | Instructor

Date Assigned | Date Completed

CHAPTER 9 Stocks

Finance Online: Comparing Blue-Chip and Income Stocks

Chapter 9 states that blue-chip stocks are issued by the strongest and most respected companies, but that companies with income stocks offer higher-than-average dividends. What is the actual difference between these two kinds of investments?

To find out, visit the Web sites of a company that issues blue-chip stock and one that issues income stock. Choose companies that the chapter designates for each kind of stock, or explore the Internet to find the names of other stocks labeled blue-chip or income. Then answer the questions below.

Keywords Used	Site Name	Web Site Addresses	Information Offered

1. List the names of the blue-chip stock company and the income stock company you researched. What are the most recent market values of their stock?

2. What dividend did the blue-chip stock pay last quarter? What did the income stock pay?

3. Assume that each company pays the same dividend for four quarters. Which company offers the higher current yield? (Remember: Current Yield = Annual Dividend ÷ Market Value)

Student　　Class　　Instructor

Date Assigned　　Date Completed

CHAPTER 9 Stocks

Software Activity (Optional)

Spreadsheet Application

Comparing the Performance of Stock Investments

OBJECTIVE: *To evaluate the performance of securities using numeric measurements for investment yield, current return, total return, capital gain, and earnings ratios.*

Practice Situation

Phillip owns the following stocks and wishes to evaluate the performance of his investments. He read recently that many stock analysts predict declining returns on pharmaceutical and medical stocks for the near future. Phillip wants to verify for himself that this trend is occurring. He presents the following data on his portfolio. Calculate the current yield, current return, capital gain, total return, earnings per share, and price-earnings ratio for both of Phillip's investments for the past two years. Compare the performance of each stock for each year and then answer the questions that follow.

Rudland Pharmaceuticals
6/1/2006–5/31/2007

Purchased 160 shares at $38/share on 6/1/2006

Annual dividends paid: $1.62 per share

Market value at 5/31/2007 = $41.00

Rudland Pharmaceuticals reported net earnings of $2,200,000 with 200,000 outstanding shares of common stock

6/1/2007–5/31/2008

Annual dividends paid: $1.55 per share

Market value at 5/31/2008 = $37.00

Rudland Pharmaceuticals reported net earnings of $2,100,000 with 220,000 outstanding shares of common stock

A & R Medical Technologies
6/1/2006–5/31/2007

Purchased 220 shares at $35.50/share on 6/1/2006

Annual dividends paid: $1.85 per share

Market value at 5/31/2007 = $38.00

A&R Medical Technologies reported net earnings of $750,000 with 100,000 outstanding shares of common stock

6/1/2007–5/31/2008

Annual dividends paid: $1.55 per share

Market value at 5/31/2008 = $36.00

A&R Medical Technologies reported net earnings of $765,000 with 120,000 outstanding shares of common stock

Spreadsheet Directions

1. Start your spreadsheet software program and open problem **SA09.xls.**
2. Using the data presented for both stocks for the period 6/1/2006–5/31/2007, calculate the following:
   - Current Yield
   - Current Return
   - Capital Gain
   - Total Return
   - Earnings per share
   - Price-earnings ratio
3. Using the data presented for the period 6/1/2007–5/31/2008, calculate the same performance measurements for both stocks.
4. Format your calculated amounts for Current Yield as a Percentage, 2 decimal places.

5. Format your calculated amounts for Current Return, Capital Gain, Total Return, and Earnings per share as Currency, 2 decimal places.

6. The price-earnings ratio amounts should be formatted to Number, 2 decimal places.

7. When you have completed your calculations, save your work to a new file labeled **SA09***.xls.** (Replace *** with your initials.)

8. Print out a copy of your work if your teacher has instructed you to do so.

Interpreting Results

1. What was the total return for Rudland Pharmaceuticals stock for the year ended 5/31/2007? For the year ended 5/31/2008? ____________________

2. Is Phillip's Rudland Pharmaceutical stock investment experiencing an increase or a decline in total return? ____________________

3. What was the current yield for A&R Medical Technology stock for the year ended 5/31/2007? For the year ended 5/31/2008? ____________________

Drawing Conclusions

1. Based on your calculations for these two years, would you agree with the opinions of the stock analysts? Are Phillip's investments experiencing a decline in performance and returns? Explain.

____

____

____

____

2. Phillip wonders whether he should consider selling his stock. What other issues should be considered as Phillip evaluates his investment returns and goals?

____

____

Student Class Instructor

Date Assigned Date Completed

CHAPTER 9 Stocks

SELF-ASSESSMENT QUIZ

DIRECTIONS: *Identify the letter of the choice that best completes the statement or answers the question.*

1. Corporations must do all the following things for their stockholders EXCEPT (A) hold an annual meeting (B) pay dividends (C) report earnings (D) provide details on sales.
2. Why do corporations split their stock? (A) to keep stockholders happy (B) to increase the stock's market value (C) to decrease the stockholders' investment (D) to set an ideal price for the stock.
3. Of the following choices, the investment with the greatest risk is (A) common stock (B) preferred stock (C) government bonds (D) a savings account.
4. Stock considered to be a conservative and safe investment is known as (A) growth stock (B) small cap stock (C) blue-chip stock (D) income stock.
5. Which company's stock do financial professionals consider a cyclical stock? (A) Home Depot (B) Ford (C) Southwest Airlines (D) General Electric.
6. For information on a company's stock prices, the most up-to-date of the following sources is (A) Kiplinger's (B) a quarterly report from company headquarters (C) the company's home page on the Internet (D) a financial report from Moody's Investor Services.
7. The current yield of an investment equals the annual dividend divided by the investment's (A) current market value (B) capital gain (C) current return (D) earnings per share.
8. An investor purchases securities from a corporation through an investment bank in a(n) (A) securities exchange (B) primary market (C) secondary market (D) over-the-counter market.
9. Which request lets an account executive decide when to buy or sell a security and at what price? (A) limit order (B) stop order (C) market order (D) discretionary order.
10. An investor can buy stock without going through an account executive by (A) reinvesting dividends (B) dollar cost averaging (C) buying on margin (D) selling short.

Student ______ **Class** ______ **Instructor** ______

Date Assigned ______ **Date Completed** ______

CHAPTER 10 Bonds and Mutual Funds

Reviewing Key Terms: Complete the Sentence

DIRECTIONS: *Using terms from the following list, complete the sentences below. Write the letter of the item you have chosen in the space provided.*

A. mortgage bond	D. revenue bond	G. net asset value (NAV)
B. serial bonds	E. investment-grade bonds	H. no-load fund
C. municipal bonds	F. closed-end fund	I. prospectus
		J. capital gain distributions

1. A state or local government issues ______to pay for ongoing activities.
2. Potential investors can find detailed information about a particular mutual fund in a report called a(n) ______.
3. Companies or municipalities with good financial stability issue ______.
4. A(n) ______ is repaid from the income generated by the project it is designed to finance.
5. The assets of a corporation are used to back a(n) ______.
6. The amount one mutual fund share is worth is called its ______.
7. The individual investor pays no commission for investing in a(n) ______.
8. ______ are issued at the same time but mature on different dates.
9. Payments made to shareholders that result from the sale of securities in a fund's portfolio are ______.
10. A(n) ______ has a fixed number of shares that are issued by an investment company when the fund is first organized.

Student Class Instructor

Date Assigned Date Completed

CHAPTER 10 Bonds and Mutual Funds

Understanding Key Concepts

DIRECTIONS: *On a separate sheet of paper, answer the questions below.*

1. What information is typically on a corporate bond?
2. Why do investors buy debenture bonds?
3. Why do investors who buy subordinated debentures usually receive higher interest rates than other bondholders?
4. Why is the interest rate on a convertible bond often lower than that on other types of corporate bonds?
5. How does a call feature benefit a corporation?
6. Perry bought bonds that the corporation is now calling. Where can Perry look to find the amount of the premium the corporation agreed to pay in case of a call?
7. Ben and Jill want to purchase bonds to finance their toddler's college education. Which kind would you recommend: Treasury bonds or bonds issued by Fannie Mae? Explain your answer.
8. Stella is looking for a safe investment that will provide a predictable source of income. She consults the Moody Bond Survey and finds the names of two corporations in which she would like to invest. One is rated B and the other Baa. Which investment will probably best meet her needs? Why?
9. How does an aggressive growth fund differ from an equity income fund?
10. Emilio wants to buy shares in an open-end mutual fund and do so in the simplest way possible. Which option would you recommend: a regular account transaction, a savings plan, or a reinvestment plan? Why?

Student Class Instructor

Date Assigned Date Completed

CHAPTER 10 Bonds and Mutual Funds

Activity 1: *Creating a Checklist for Evaluating a Bond*

SCANS COMPETENCIES ACHIEVED

Reading, Writing, Math, Acquiring and evaluating information, Organizing and maintaining information, Interpreting and communicating information, Teaching others

OBJECTIVE: *Prepare a checklist to use to evaluate a bond investment.*

Imagine you saved $1,000 and wanted to invest it in some kind of bond. What would you need to know to make a wise investment? In this activity you will prepare a checklist of elements that you would need to examine in order to evaluate the return, risk, and suitability of a particular bond. Then you'll exchange checklists with a partner and use your partner's checklist to evaluate an actual bond.

Use the space below to make notes. Then, on a separate sheet of paper, create a checklist of elements that should be examined when evaluating a bond. Make sure you leave enough space for the answers. Exchange checklists with a partner. Finally, choose a specific corporate, municipal, or Treasury bond; look it up in one of the sources listed in the chapter; and fill in your partner's checklist with information from the source.

Student Class Instructor

Date Assigned Date Completed

CHAPTER 10 Bonds and Mutual Funds

Activity 2: *Analyzing Mutual Funds*

SCANS COMPETENCIES ACHIEVED

Reading, Writing, Problem solving, Decision making, Reasoning, Acquiring and evaluating information, Interpreting and communicating information, Organizing and maintaining information, Selecting technology, Applying technology to task

OBJECTIVE: *Obtain information about three mutual funds, analyze the information, and profile a suitable investor for one of the funds.*

The revolution in computer technology and the Internet have placed a vast amount of up-to-the-minute information at the fingertips of anyone with a computer and a modem. This especially benefits investors in mutual funds. In this activity, you'll choose three mutual funds to evaluate. Then write a short profile of the ideal investor in one of the funds you evaluated.

First, choose three different mutual funds with different focuses (for example, a large-cap growth fund, a small-cap fund, and an international fund). Then check financial publications at the library, a financial Web site, or the company Web sites. You could also check a newspaper that features a mutual fund section. Enter information about the funds in the chart on the next page. Finally, based on the data you obtain, as well as what you have learned in the text about risk, investment objectives, and financial goal setting, write a short description of the kind of investor you feel is suitable for one of the funds you have investigated.

Investor Profile for:

Fund name			
Family			
Type/Objective			
Charges (if any)			
Current NAV			
Major holdings			
Return			
1-year return			
3-year return			
5-year return			
Other data			

Student | Class | Instructor

Date Assigned | Date Completed

CHAPTER 10 Bonds and Mutual Funds

Math-Building Skills: Many Happy Returns

OBJECTIVE: *Determine the total returns for a mutual fund.*

A key to being an intelligent investor is knowing how well your investments are doing. Part of this knowledge is the total return over several time periods. In this activity, you'll use your math skills to determine the 1-, 2-, 3-, and 5-year total returns for a mutual fund investment.

The total return for a selected period is determined by subtracting the net asset value listed for the period from the current value, then dividing the difference by the net asset value of the period. For example, suppose that the current net asset value is $46.98, and one year ago it was $42.46. To find the 1-year total return, subtract $42.46 from $46.98. The result is $4.52. Divide $4.52 by $42.46. The total return for the 1-year period is 10.6%.

To find the average annual return for two or more years, divide the percentage gain or loss by the number of years in the period. The average annual return for the 1-year period would be 10.6 (the percentage gain) divided by 1 (the number of years in the period), so the answer would be 10.6%. Don't forget to adjust your figures for negative numbers, which result in years when funds have losses.

DIRECTIONS: *The following chart shows some financial data for the New Directions Small Cap Discovery Fund. Use the data shown to determine the total returns for the periods listed. Use the space below the chart for your computations.*

Period	Net Asset Value (NAV)	Total Return for Period	Average Annual Return for Period
Current	$46.98	—	—
1 year ago	$42.46	10.6%	10.6%
2 years ago	$38.90	______	______
3 years ago	$45.92	______	______
5 years ago	$31.67	______	______

Student _______________ Class _______________ Instructor _______________

Date Assigned _______________ Date Completed _______________

CHAPTER 10 Bonds and Mutual Funds

Your Financial Portfolio Worksheet

Evaluating Mutual Funds

Because a mutual fund can sometimes earn a higher return than a CD, you might want to invest your money in a mutual fund someday. Doing your research before you invest can help you make a wise choice. Practice researching mutual funds by picking one of the following:

- Fidelity Magellan Fund
- AIM Blue Chip Fund Class A
- Your own choice

Then call the investment company for a prospectus of the mutual fund that you've chosen. You can also check the Morningstar Web site or find *Morningstar Mutual Funds* at your local library. Fill in the information on the checklist below to evaluate the fund.

Comparing Mutual Funds

1. Name of mutual fund _______________
2. Mutual fund type (stock, bond, futures, money market, balanced, indexed, sector, etc.) _______________
3. Mutual fund objective (aggressive growth, moderate growth, income and safety, and income) _______________
4. Number of securities in fund's portfolio _______________
5. Types of industries in fund's portfolio _______________
6. Yield in the last 12 months _______________
7. Average return or yield for the last 5 years _______________
8. Average return or yield for the last 10 years _______________
9. Fees: load, 12b-1 fee, annual management fee _______________
10. What is the minimum investment? _______________
11. Is the fund closed to new investors? _______________
12. Morningstar rating (in stars and risk) _______________

Student Class Instructor

Date Assigned Date Completed

If you had money to invest, would you invest in the mutual fund? Explain why or why not. Write your answer in the space provided below.

Student Class Instructor

Date Assigned Date Completed

CHAPTER 10 Bonds and Mutual Funds

Finance Online: Fund Ratings

Ratings for mutual funds are provided by services such as Standard & Poor's; Lipper Analytical Services; Morningstar, Inc.; Value Line; and Wiesenberger Investment Companies. A mutual fund rating shows how a fund performed in relation to other mutual funds in the same category. These services also provide other information about mutual funds. Some provide graphs to show the growth or list the annual returns in chart form. They might list the holdings of each fund, the manager of the fund, the minimum investment, sales charges, and long-term performance.

Use the Internet to find the names of four specific funds and how they are rated. Use one of the major rating services as a keyword. Go to a Web site that gives fund ratings. Use the information you find to answer the questions below.

Keywords Used	Site Name	Web Site Addresses	Information Offered

1. In addition to ratings, what other information does the site provide about the mutual fund?

2. List the names of four funds with different ratings. Write the rating after each fund.

3. Of the four funds you listed, which would you most likely invest in? Explain your reasoning.

Student | Class | Instructor

Date Assigned | Date Completed

CHAPTER 10 Bonds and Mutual Funds

Software Activity (Optional)

Spreadsheet Application

Calculating Profit or Loss on a Bond Transaction

OBJECTIVE: *To calculate the profit or loss realized on a bond transaction.*

Practice Situation

Assume that you purchased an 8⅜ percent Phoenix Municipal Water Bond on December 1, 2000. You paid $650 plus a $25 commission charge, for a total investment of $675. The bond holds a maturity date of 2020. On December 1, 2010, you sold the bond at its current market value of $1,050. Complete the spreadsheet to determine the total profit or loss on the bond transaction. Then, answer the questions that follow.

Purchase Costs	
1 bond @ $650	
Plus commission cost	
Total investment	

Returns when Sold	
1 bond @ $1,050	
Minus commission fee	
Total return on sale	

Transaction Summary	
Total return on sale	
Minus total investment	
Profit from bond sale	
Plus interest	
Total profit and interest on transaction	

Spreadsheet Directions

1. Start your spreadsheet software program and open problem **SA10.xls.**
2. Using the data presented, first input the purchase costs for the bond. Format all dollar amounts to Number, 2 decimal places. Use 1000 Separator (,).
3. Next, input the data for the dollar returns on the sale of the bond.
4. Complete the transaction summary information. When computing the interest on the bond, remember to multiply the annual interest earned by the number of years that the bond has been held.
5. When you have completed your spreadsheet, save your work to a new file labeled **SA10***.xls.** (Replace *** with your initials.)
6. Print out a copy of your work if your teacher has instructed you to do so.

Interpreting Results

1. What was your total investment for the bond on December 1, 2006? ____________________
2. What were the total dollar returns on the sale of the bond on December 1, 2016? ____________________
3. What total interest income was earned on the bond for the period of 12/1/2006 through 12/1/2016? ____________________
4. What total profit and interest was earned on the bond transaction? ____________________

Drawing Conclusions

1. In this example, the Phoenix Municipal Water bond was sold well in advance of its maturity date. If the bond had been held until its maturity date, what total interest would have been earned over the life of the bond?

2. What factors might cause an investor to sell a bond prior to its maturity date? How might fluctuations in the overall interest rates of the economy impact bond market values? Explain.

Student Class Instructor

Date Assigned Date Completed

CHAPTER 10 Bonds and Mutual Funds

SELF-ASSESSMENT QUIZ

DIRECTIONS: *Identify the letter of the choice that best completes the statement or answers the question.*

1. The face value of a bond is the amount a bondholder (A) pays for the bond (B) receives at maturity (C) receives in interest (D) loses if the corporation fails.
2. Assets of a corporation may be sold to repay a (A) mortgage bond (B) debenture (C) convertible bond (D) bond indenture.
3. An additional amount that a company pays above the value of its bond is called (A) a sinking fund (B) a coupon (C) a premium (D) an interest check.
4. Only the bond owner can collect interest from a (A) registered bond (B) registered coupon bond (C) bearer bond (D) zero-coupon bond.
5. Which investment offers the highest rate of interest? (A) Treasury bill (B) Treasury bond (C) Series EE Savings Bond (D) agency bond
6. Municipal bonds are offered by all the following levels of government EXCEPT (A) federal (B) state (C) county (D) city.
7. The lowest Standard & Poor's rating a bond can have and still be considered investment grade is (A) B (B) BB (C) BBB (D) C.
8. How do you find the current yield of a bond? (A) Divide the bond's current market value by the amount of annual interest income. (B) Divide the amount of annual interest income by the bond's current market value. (C) Multiply the face value times the annual rate of interest. (D) Multiply the face value times the rate of return.
9. A back-end load on a mutual fund is charged for (A) each purchase of shares (B) managing the mutual fund (C) marketing and advertising the fund (D) withdrawing money from the fund.
10. Investors pay penalty fees if they fail to make regular purchases of shares when investing in a mutual fund under a (A) regular account transaction (B) voluntary savings plan (C) contractual savings plan (D) reinvestment plan.

Student Class Instructor

Date Assigned Date Completed

CHAPTER 11 Real Estate and Other Investment Alternatives

Reviewing Key Terms: Complete the Sentence

DIRECTIONS: *Using terms from the following list, complete the sentences below. Write the letter of the term you have chosen in the space provided.*

A. direct investment	D. syndicate	G. financial leverage
B. commercial property	E. limited partner	H. precious metals
C. indirect investment	F. participation certificate	I. precious gems
		J. collectibles

1. An investment in a group of mortgages that have been purchased by a government agency is a(n) ______.
2. A trustee is appointed to hold legal title to a property on behalf of an investor or group of investors in a(n) ______.
3. The owner holds legal title to the property he or she purchased in a(n) ______.
4. Valuable ores, such as gold, platinum, and silver are examples of ______.
5. Rough mineral deposits that miners dig from the earth and that jewelers cut into brilliant jewels are ______.
6. A(n) ______ is a temporary association of individuals or business firms organized to perform a task that requires a large amount of funds.
7. The use of borrowed funds for investment purposes is called ______.
8. Rare coins, rare books, stamps, paintings, and other such items are known as ______.
9. A(n) ______ is liable only for the amount of his or her investment in the business.
10. Land or a building that produces lease or rental income is a(n) ______.

Student Class Instructor

Date Assigned Date Completed

CHAPTER 11 Real Estate and Other Investment Alternatives

Understanding Key Concepts

DIRECTIONS: On a separate sheet of paper, answer the questions below.

1. What financial advantage does a person who has a home mortgage enjoy?
2. Antonio bought a small apartment house and collects rent from three tenants. He would like to buy a larger apartment house and collect even more money. When do many investors start buying larger properties?
3. Michelle wants to invest in real estate but does not have enough money to buy property on her own. She has heard of hybrid Real Estate Investment Trusts and wants to know what they are. How would you explain them to her?
4. Explain how a limited partnership works. Include the terms *general partner, limited partners,* and *participation units.*
5. List four regulations that the federal government requires real estate investments trusts (REITs) to follow.
6. Why are participation certificates risk-free real estate investments?
7. Peter has $10,000 to invest but will need it in six months to pay for college tuition. Would you recommend that he use his money to buy land? Why or why not?
8. What must an investor do to make a profit from investing in precious metals?
9. What are the risks of investing in gemstones?
10. Compare the collecting process before and after the introduction of auctions on the Internet.

Student ______ Class ______ Instructor ______

Date Assigned ______ Date Completed ______

CHAPTER 11 Real Estate and Other Investment Alternatives

Activity 1: *Collecting*

SCANS COMPETENCIES ACHIEVED

Writing, Listening, Speaking, Acquiring and evaluating information, Interpreting and communicating information

OBJECTIVE: *Conduct a survey on the collecting activities of relatives and friends.*

Chances are, many of your relatives and friends collect something. What they collect could run the gamut from Beanie Babies and Barbie dolls to Civil War weapons and early farm tools. Prepare a survey to find out what three different people collect, why they chose that particular kind of collectible, how much money (if any) they estimate they have made from their collectibles, and what predictions they can offer about the future worth of the collectibles they specialize in. Use the space at the bottom of this page to make notes about whom to contact. Tabulate your survey results on a separate sheet of paper and share them with the class. Then discuss which collectibles, if any, seem to be a good investment compared to stocks, bonds, real estate, and other categories.

Student ______ Class ______ Instructor ______

Date Assigned ______ Date Completed ______

CHAPTER 11 Real Estate and Other Investment Alternatives

Activity 2: *Real Estate Investments and Inflation*

SCANS COMPETENCIES ACHIEVED

Reading, Writing, Math, Acquiring and evaluating information, Organizing and maintaining information, Interpreting and communicating information, Selecting technology, Applying technology to task

OBJECTIVE: *Research and evaluate the rise in overall costs and the rise in housing costs.*

In this chapter you learned about the advantages and disadvantages of investing in real estate, either directly or indirectly. Would real estate have been a good investment over the last ten years? To figure this out, you need to compare the rise in the cost of housing to the inflation rate.

Look in a world almanac or other reference resource to find the rise in the consumer price index (the standard measure of inflation) for the years 1990–1999. You can also find information on the Internet; the Web site of the Bureau of Labor Statistics of the Department of Labor is a good place to start. Enter these figures in the first column on the next page. Then use the same or another source to find the average yearly increase for the same years for housing. If you were a real estate investor, these figures would reflect how much the value of your property had increased. Write these figures in the second column.

When you have recorded the information, use the graph grid to create a line graph showing the changes in both sets of data during the 1990s.

CPI % Increase		Shelter Cost % Increase	
1990	______	1990	______
1991	______	1991	______
1992	______	1992	______
1993	______	1993	______
1994	______	1994	______
1995	______	1995	______
1996	______	1996	______
1997	______	1997	______
1998	______	1998	______
1999	______	1999	______

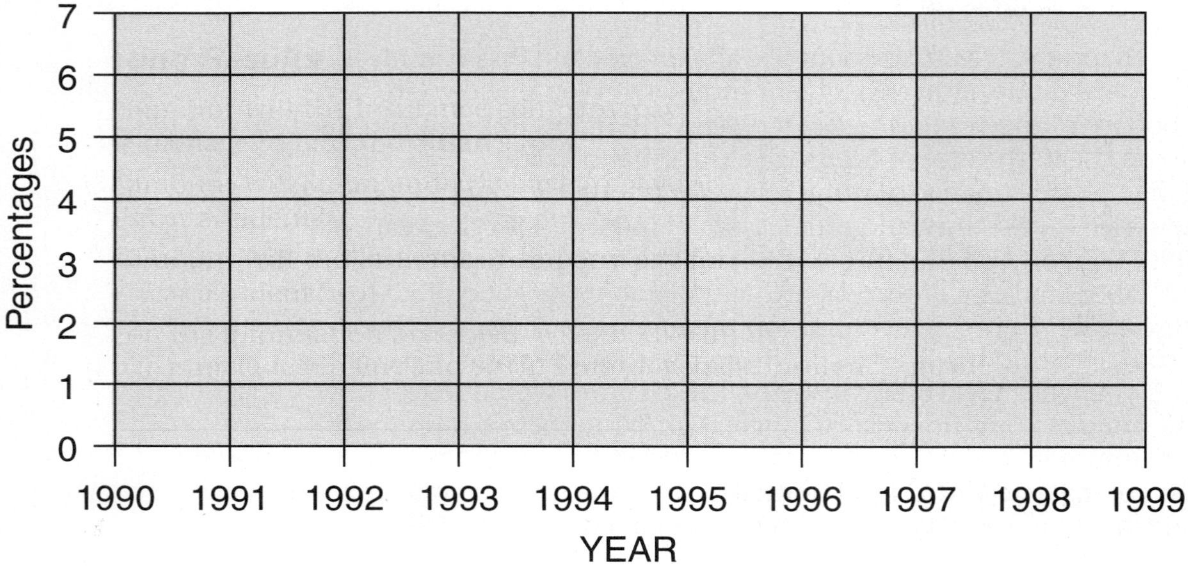

Would real estate have been a good investment during the 1990s? Why or why not?

____

____

____

____

____

____

____

____

____

Student ______ Class ______ Instructor ______

Date Assigned ______ Date Completed ______

CHAPTER 11 Real Estate and Other Investment Alternatives

Math-Building Skills: Analyze the Return on a Real Estate Investment

Felice bought a duplex apartment at a cost of $150,000. Her mortgage payments on the property are $940 per month, $121 of which can be deducted from her income taxes. Her real estate taxes total $1,440 per year, and insurance costs her $900 per year. She estimates that she will spend $1,000 each year per apartment for maintenance costs. The tenants will pay for all utilities.

DIRECTIONS: *In the space below, use this information to figure out the rent Felice must charge for each apartment to break even.*

1. What monthly rent must she charge for each apartment to break even?

______

______

______

______

______

______

2. What must she charge to make $2,000 in profit each year?

______

Student ____________ Class ____________ Instructor ____________

Date Assigned ____________ Date Completed ____________

CHAPTER 11 Real Estate and Other Investment Alternatives

Your Financial Portfolio Worksheet

Collectibles

1. List five things you could collect that will keep their value or possibly be worth more in the future.

a. ____________

b. ____________

c. ____________

d. ____________

e. ____________

2. Choose one and describe why it appeals to you.

____

____

____

3. Explain how the experts appraise its value:

a. Age: ____________

b. Quality: ____________

c. Rarity: ____________

d. Popular demand: ____________

4. Why would this collectible be interesting for you to keep?

____

____

____

5. Do you think it would be a good or bad long-term investment? Why?

____

____

____

Student ______________________ Class __________ Instructor __________

Date Assigned ______________________ Date Completed ______________________

CHAPTER 11 Real Estate and Other Investment Alternatives

Finance Online: Collecting Online

How valuable can a sports card get? In 2000, a baseball card featuring Honus Wagner, a Pittsburgh Pirate from the 1900s, sold for $1.1 million. A more recent card—a picture of Mickey Mantle issued by the Topps Card Company in 1952—was valued at $16,000 in 1999.

Most baseball cards will never command these prices, but because the initial investment is about twenty cents, the rate of return on many cards can be huge. For this activity, use an Internet search engine to find other valuable baseball cards. Visit as many Web sites as necessary to find answers to the items.

Keywords Used	Site Names	Web Site Addresses	Information Offered

1. Name two players with cards valued at more than $20. Also note the names of the companies that issued the cards, the years of the cards, and the cards' prices.

____

____

2. List three other kinds of baseball memorabilia sold on the Internet.

____

____

3. What other sports have collectible cards offered on the Internet?

____

____

Student | Class | Instructor

Date Assigned | Date Completed

CHAPTER 11 Real Estate and Other Investment Alternatives

Software Activity (Optional)

Spreadsheet Application

Choosing Investment Alternatives

OBJECTIVE: *To compare and assess the potential rewards and risks associated with investment alternatives.*

Practice Situation

Raju's parents gave him $2,000 as a graduation gift. He is very interested in the real estate industry and wonders whether he could invest in that area.

His father suggests that Raju might invest his money in a mutual fund participation certificate. He can buy into a mutual fund offered by the Federal Home Loan Mortgage Corporation for $2,000. He will be charged a 1% commission on the purchase of the certificate. The guaranteed return on this investment is 5.5% annually. Raju plans to cash out any interest he earns in the mutual fund as it is paid to him. Assume the participation certificate will increase in value by 11% in 4 years.

As a second alternative, Raju researched the possible purchase of Oracle Corporation common stock, currently selling at $80 per share. Recent news featured the Oracle Internet platform and forecasted heavy use by Web developers worldwide. Oracle paid dividends of $3.87 per share for the last year. Assuming this dividend will be paid at the same level over the next 4 years, calculate the annual dollar returns that Raju can expect for this option. Raju will have to pay a $50 fee for this stock purchase. In researching this stock, he finds that Oracle stock has increased in value by 6% every year for the past 5 years. Assume that the Oracle stock value continues to increase by 6% each year.

Complete the spreadsheet shown on page 127 to help Raju analyze his investment opportunities and potential returns.

Student | Class | Instructor

Date Assigned | Date Completed

Investment costs:	Mutual Fund Participation Certificate	Oracle Stock
Investment amount		
Plus Commission		
Total Investment Costs		
Annual Anticipated Returns:		
Annual interest or dividend earned Year 1		
Annual interest or dividend earned Year 2		
Annual interest or dividend earned Year 3		
Annual interest or dividend earned Year 4		
Total earned		
Potential Value at Year 4:		
Market Value of investment at Year 4		
Summary Information:		
Potential selling price		
Less investment cost		
Profit from sale of investment		
Plus interest or dividend returns		
Potential profit and interest from transaction		

Spreadsheet Directions

1. Start your spreadsheet software program and open problem **SA11.xls.**
2. Record Raju's costs involved with each investment opportunity, to determine his total investment costs.
3. Next, compute the annual returns expected for each investment. Remember that Raju does not intend to reinvest interest earnings.
4. To compute the potential value of each investment at Year 4, review the data presented for the anticipated increase for the mutual fund and the stock. Insert formulas to compute these increases in value.
5. Finally, determine the potential profits and interest from each transaction based on the data presented.

6. Perform your calculations and complete the spreadsheet, then save your work to a new file labeled **SA11***.xls.** (Replace *** with your initials.)

7. Print out a copy of your work if your teacher has instructed you to do so.

Interpreting Results

1. How many shares of Oracle stock could Raju purchase with his graduation gift?

2. What would the total investment cost be for the mutual fund participation certificate?

3. What amount of dividend income does Raju expect to earn over the 4 years that he plans to hold the shares of Oracle stock?

4. If the assumption for each investment's potential value were realized, what total profit and interest for each investment would be earned?

Drawing Conclusions

1. Assuming that Raju wants to invest his money in an investment that carries less risk, which investment would you recommend? Explain.

Student Class Instructor

Date Assigned Date Completed

2. Before Raju invests his money, list the types of research that Raju should do to investigate his investment interests. What sources of information would help Raju make an informed decision?

Student Class Instructor

Date Assigned Date Completed

CHAPTER 11 Real Estate and Other Investments

SELF-ASSESSMENT QUIZ

DIRECTIONS: *Circle the letter of the choice that best completes the statement or answers the question.*

1. An example of a direct investment is a (A) home mortgage (B) real estate syndicate (C) real estate investment trust (D) Ginnie Mae certificate.
2. In a syndicate organized as a limited partnership, responsibility for all the partnership's liabilities belongs to the (A) limited partners (B) general partner (C) tenants (D) federal government.
3. An investment in a real estate syndicate can be (A) depreciable (B) deductible (C) tax-exempt (D) diversified.
4. REITs might invest the participants' money in any of the following items EXCEPT (A) construction loans (B) financial instruments (C) properties (D) mortgages.
5. Which of the following are examples of participation certificates? (A) Maes and Macs (B) U.S. Treasury Bonds (C) REITs (D) real estate syndicates
6. Generally, an indirect investment in real estate is (A) easily converted into cash (B) a hedge against inflation (C) only for the wealthy (D) a good tax shelter.
7. The price of gold might fall when (A) war threatens (B) the government seems unstable (C) countries make peace (D) inflation soars.
8. In the year 2003, which of the following precious metals was most valuable? (A) gold (B) platinum (C) palladium (D) rhodium
9. Eighty-five percent of the world's supply of rough diamonds comes from (A) the United States (B) Great Britain (C) South Africa (D) China.
10. Drawbacks of finding collectibles on the Internet include the (A) inability to comparison shop (B) lack of a wide range of sellers (C) inability to examine items for flaws (D) frequently charged buyer's commissions.

Student ______ Class ______ Instructor ______

Date Assigned ______ Date Completed ______

CHAPTER 12 Planning Your Tax Strategy

Reviewing Key Terms: Complete the Sentence

DIRECTIONS: *Using terms from the following list, complete the sentences below. Write the letter of the term you have chosen in the space provided.*

A. excise tax	D. interest income	G. itemized deduction
B. gift tax	E. dividend income	H. tax credit
C. earned income	F. standard deduction	I. allowance
		J. tax audit

1. A(n) ______ is collected on money or property valued at more than $10,000, given by one person to another in a single year.
2. ______ is the amount set by the Internal Revenue Service on which no taxes are paid.
3. Federal and state governments collect a(n) ______ on specific goods and services, such as gasoline, air travel, and telephone service.
4. A detailed examination of a person's tax return by the Internal Revenue Service is called a(n) ______.
5. The money a person receives from a bank, credit union, or savings and loan for keeping his or her money there is ______.
6. A(n) ______ is subtracted directly from the amount of taxes that a person owes.
7. The cash dividend a person receives from investments is called ______.
8. The money a person receives for working is ______.
9. A specific expense that a person can subtract from his or her adjusted gross income is a(n) ______.
10. A(n) ______ is an adjustment to the tax withheld from your paycheck, based on your marital status and whether you have dependents.

Student Class Instructor

Date Assigned Date Completed

CHAPTER 12 Planning Your Tax Strategy

Understanding Key Concepts

DIRECTIONS: *On a separate sheet of paper, answer the questions below.*

1. List six of the many government services that are paid for with taxes.
2. Name the four categories of items on which people pay taxes.
3. How are the taxes on employees' earnings collected?
4. What is the difference between gross income, adjusted gross income, and taxable income? Write a formula for calculating a person's adjusted gross income (AGI) and another formula for calculating his or her taxable income.
5. Compare and contrast standard deductions, itemized deductions, exemptions, and tax credits. Give an example of each.
6. Victor is a 20-year-old American citizen who lives with his parents and goes to college part-time. Does he qualify as a dependent on his parents' tax return?
7. Jamie cannot file her tax return by the April 15 due date. What should she do?
8. Ryan has a wife, two children, and a mortgage. He made less than $50,000 this year. Because his job does not provide insurance, he had to pay out of his own pocket for the delivery of his younger child in June. Would you recommend that he use Form 1040A or Form 1040 when filing his taxes? Explain.
9. Teri is being audited by the IRS. Offer what you consider the three most helpful tips to make the audit go more smoothly.
10. Bart made $40,000 in adjusted gross income this year. He spent $200 on union dues, $500 on job-related education, and $200 on business tools. How much of these job-related expenses can he deduct? Explain.

Student Class Instructor

Date Assigned Date Completed

CHAPTER 12 Planning Your Tax Strategy

Activity 1: *Looking for Help*

SCANS COMPETENCIES ACHIEVED
Writing, Listening, Speaking, Acquiring and evaluating information

OBJECTIVE: *Survey local tax-preparation organizations to find out their costs and services.*

Completing tax returns can be complicated and confusing. Numerous commercial and volunteer organizations exist to help you. Some charge a fee, while others are staffed by volunteers and are free. Use the chart below to compile information on three tax-preparation organizations in your community. At least one should be a free service. In the Cost/Service column, note which forms are included in the base rate. In the Eligibility column, note who may use the service, if there are restrictions.

Name of firm	Cost/Services	Eligibility

Student Class Instructor

Date Assigned Date Completed

CHAPTER 12 Planning Your Tax Strategy

Activity 2: *Knowing Where to Look for Information*

SCANS COMPETENCIES ACHIEVED

Reading, Writing, Knowing how to learn, Acquiring and evaluating information, Organizing and maintaining information, Participating as a member of a team

OBJECTIVE: *Work in a group to assemble an annotated source list of tax information.*

Knowing where to turn for information about filing your tax return and planning a tax strategy is extremely useful. This activity will give you the chance to work in a small group to put together a list of at least 10 good sources of tax information, including books, publications from the IRS, Web sites, tax-preparation software, and other materials. Use your imagination to track down materials. As always, the community library is a good place to start; most have extensive tax information sections. Use the space at the bottom of this page to make notes, make group assignments, and organize your findings. Then use the chart on the next page to present your information.

Student Class Instructor

Date Assigned Date Completed

Title	Type of Resource	Notes

Student Class Instructor

Date Assigned Date Completed

CHAPTER 12 Planning Your Tax Strategy

Math-Building Skills: A Tax Pie

OBJECTIVE: *Create a pie chart that shows how much of each kind of tax a typical person pays.*

You've probably wondered how much total tax, and what kinds of taxes, you might have to pay as your financial life becomes more complicated. A good way to see quickly the distribution of a person's taxes is to make a pie chart. In this activity, you'll use your drafting skills or graphing software to make a chart based on the information below. Create a pie chart that shows in percentages the taxes that Adam Moorehead paid in a recent year.

federal income tax	$5,380	excise taxes	$177
state income tax	$612	real estate taxes	$638
city income tax	$199	Social Security tax	$1,356
sales taxes	$735	Medicare tax	$319

Student ______________________ Class ______________ Instructor ______________

Date Assigned ______________________ Date Completed ______________________

CHAPTER 12 Planning Your Tax Strategy

Your Financial Portfolio Worksheet

W-2 to 1040EZ

Complete your income tax return, using this sample Form 1040EZ. Assume that your wages for the year were $13,220 and you earned $137 in interest from your savings account. Your W-2 form shows that you had $1,003 in federal income tax withheld. Your parents cannot claim you on their income tax return. Find your tax in the tax table below and calculate your refund or amount you owe.

Tax Table

20-- Tax Table

For persons with taxable income of less than $50,000

Example. Mr. Brown is single. His taxable income on line 6 of Form 1040EZ is $26,250. First, he finds the $26,250–26,300 income line. Next, he finds the "Single" column and reads down the column. The amount shown where the income line and filing status column meet → is $4,010. This is the tax amount he should enter on line 10 of Form 1040EZ.

At least	But less than	Single	Married filing jointly
		Your tax is—	
26,200	26,250	3,996	3,934
26,250	26,300	(4,010)	3,941
26,300	26,350	4,024	3,949
26,350	26,400	4,038	3,956

If Form 1040EZ, line 6, is—		And you are—		If Form 1040EZ, line 6, is—		And you are—		If Form 1040EZ, line 6, is—		And you are—	
At least	But less than	Single	Married filing jointly	At least	But less than	Single	Married filing jointly	At least	But less than	Single	Married filing jointly
		Your tax is—				Your tax is—				Your tax is—	
4,000				**5,000**				**6,000**			
4,000	4,050	604	604	5,000	5,050	754	754	6,000	6,050	904	904
4,050	4,100	611	611	5,050	5,100	761	761	6,050	6,100	911	911
4,100	4,150	619	619	5,100	5,150	769	769	6,100	6,150	919	919
4,150	4,200	626	626	5,150	5,200	776	776	6,150	6,200	926	926
4,200	4,250	634	634	5,200	5,250	784	784	6,200	6,250	934	934
4,250	4,300	641	641	5,250	5,300	791	791	6,250	6,300	941	941
4,300	4,350	649	649	5,300	5,350	799	799	6,300	6,350	949	949
4,350	4,400	656	656	5,350	5,400	806	806	6,350	6,400	956	956
4,400	4,450	664	664	5,400	5,450	814	814	6,400	6,450	964	964
4,450	4,500	671	671	5,450	5,500	821	821	6,450	6,500	971	971
4,500	4,550	679	679	5,500	5,550	829	829	6,500	6,550	979	979
4,550	4,600	686	686	5,550	5,600	836	836	6,550	6,600	986	986
4,600	4,650	694	694	5,600	5,650	844	844	6,600	6,650	994	994
4,650	4,700	701	701	5,650	5,700	851	851	6,650	6,700	1,001	1,001
4,700	4,750	709	709	5,700	5,750	859	859	6,700	6,750	1,009	1,009
4,750	4,800	716	716	5,750	5,800	866	866	6,750	6,800	1,016	1,016
4,800	4,850	724	724	5,800	5,850	874	874	6,800	6,850	1,024	1,024
4,850	4,900	731	731	5,850	5,900	881	881	6,850	6,900	1,031	1,031
4,900	4,950	739	739	5,900	5,950	889	889	6,900	6,950	1,039	1,039
4,950	5,000	746	746	5,950	6,000	896	896	6,950	7,000	1,046	1,046

Form **1040EZ**

Department of the Treasury—Internal Revenue Service

Income Tax Return for Single and Joint Filers With No Dependents (99) 20--

OMB No. 1545-0675

Label (See page 14.) **Use the IRS label.** Otherwise, please print or type.

LABEL HERE

Your first name and initial	Last name		Your social security number
If a joint return, spouse's first name and initial	Last name		Spouse's social security number
Home address (number and street). If you have a P.O. box, see page 14.		Apt. no.	
City, town or post office, state, and ZIP code. If you have a foreign address, see page 14.			

▲ Important! ▲ You **must** enter your SSN(s) above.

Presidential Election Campaign (page 14)

Note. Checking "Yes" will not change your tax or reduce your refund. Do you, or your spouse if a joint return, want $3 to go to this fund? . . . . . ▶ You ☐ Yes ☐ No Spouse ☐ Yes ☐ No

Income

Attach Form(s) W-2 here. Enclose, but do not attach, any payment.

Note. You **must** check Yes or No.

1	Total wages, salaries, and tips. This should be shown in box 1 of your W-2 form(s). Attach your W-2 form(s).	1	
2	Taxable interest. If the total is over $1,500, you cannot use Form 1040EZ.	2	
3	Unemployment compensation and Alaska Permanent Fund dividends (see page 16).	3	
4	Add lines 1, 2, and 3. This is your **adjusted gross income.**	4	
5	Can your parents (or someone else) claim you on their return? **Yes.** ☐ Enter amount from worksheet on back. **No.** ☐ If **single,** enter $7,700. If **married,** enter $13,850. See back for explanation.	5	
6	Subtract line 5 from line 4. If line 5 is larger than line 4, enter -0-. This is your **taxable income.** ▶	6	

Payments and tax

7	Federal income tax withheld from box 2 of your W-2 form(s).	7	
8	**Earned income credit (EIC).**	8	
9	Add lines 7 and 8. These are your **total payments.** ▶	9	
10	**Tax.** Use the amount on **line 6 above** to find your tax in the tax table on pages 25–29 of the booklet. Then, enter the tax from the table on this line.	10	

Refund

Have it directly deposited! See page 21 and fill in 11b, 11c, and 11d.

11a	If line 9 is larger than line 10, subtract line 10 from line 9. This is your **refund.** ▶	11a	
▶ b	Routing number ☐☐☐☐☐☐☐☐☐ ▶ c Type: ☐ Checking ☐ Savings		
▶ d	Account number ☐☐☐☐☐☐☐☐☐☐☐☐☐☐☐☐☐		

Amount you owe

12	If line 10 is larger than line 9, subtract line 9 from line 10. This is the **amount you owe.** For details on how to pay, see page 22. ▶	12	

Third party designee

Do you want to allow another person to discuss this return with the IRS (see page 22)? ☐ **Yes.** Complete the following. ☐ **No**

Designee's name ▶ Phone no. ▶ ( ) Personal identification number (PIN) ▶ ☐☐☐☐☐

Sign here

Joint return? See page 13. Keep a copy for your records.

Under penalties of perjury, I declare that I have examined this return, and to the best of my knowledge and belief, it is true, correct, and accurately lists all amounts and sources of income I received during the tax year. Declaration of preparer (other than the taxpayer) is based on all information of which the preparer has any knowledge.

Your signature	Date	Your occupation	Daytime phone number ( )
Spouse's signature. If a joint return, **both** must sign.	Date	Spouse's occupation	

Paid preparer's use only

Preparer's signature ▶	Date	Check if self-employed ☐	Preparer's SSN or PTIN
Firm's name (or yours if self-employed), address, and ZIP code ▶		EIN	
		Phone no. ( )	

For Disclosure, Privacy Act, and Paperwork Reduction Act Notice, see page 24. Cat. No. 11329W Form **1040EZ** (20--)

Student Class Instructor

Date Assigned Date Completed

CHAPTER 12 Planning Your Tax Strategy

Finance Online: Cutting Taxes

The object of planning a tax strategy is to pay your fair share and no more. This usually involves tax-cutting strategies. The Internet includes a treasure trove of advice on how to cut taxes.

How can taxpayers stop paying too much in taxes? They can start planning now for next year's tax return. For this activity, use an Internet search engine to find tax-cutting strategies. Visit as many Web sites as necessary to find answers to the questions.

Keywords Used	Site Name	Web Site Addresses	Information Offered

1. How can a computer program help someone prepare to file next year's tax return?

____

____

2. What tax benefits are available for college students?

____

____

3. How can well-to-do taxpayers lower the taxes on their estates?

____

____

Student	Class	Instructor
Date Assigned	Date Completed	

CHAPTER 12 Planning Your Tax Strategy

Software Activity (Optional)

Spreadsheet Application

Computing Taxable Income and Tax Liabilities

OBJECTIVE: *To evaluate financial data in order to compute taxable income and tax liabilities.*

Practice Situation

Shelly Calloway is a CPA and prepares income tax returns for several clients. Her clients have dropped off their income and expense data to her, and she has organized the information in the following manner as she prepares to complete their returns. Compute the adjusted gross income and tax due or tax refund amounts for Shelly's clients.

	Greg Miller	Cheryl Stafford	Valerie Bowman
Gross income	$48,000.00	$55,000.00	$33,500.00
Interest earned on savings	165.00	263.00	0.00
Standard deduction amount	7,850.00	6,900.00	4,700.00
IRA deduction	3,000.00	3,000.00	0.00
Child care tax credit	800.00	580.00	0.00
Medical expenses	0.00	5,950.00	0.00
Gifts to charity	0.00	4,525.00	0.00
Real Estate taxes	0.00	2,840.00	0.00
Federal income tax withheld	11,542.39	8,260.26	3,955.98
Dependents other than self	3	2	0
Exemption amounts	12,000.00	9,000.00	3,000.00
Filing Status	Married, filing joint return	Head of household	Single

Use the following tax rates to compute taxes owed:

Tax Rate	Single Taxpayer	Married Taxpayers	Head of Household
15%	$6,000–$27,950	$12,000–$46,700	$10,000–$37,450
27%	$27,950–$67,700	$46,700–$112,850	$37,450–$96,700

Student | Class | Instructor

Date Assigned | Date Completed

	Greg Miller	Cheryl Stafford	Valerie Bowman
Adjusted Gross Income Computation			
Gross Income			
Plus Taxable Income			
Total Income			
Less IRA Deductions			
Adjusted Gross Income			
Tax Computation			
Adjusted Gross Income			
Less Itemized Deduction or Standard Deduction Amount			
Less Exemptions Amount			
Taxable Income			
Tax			
Less Tax Credits			
Total Tax			
Tax Withheld			
Tax Due			
Tax Refund Due			

Computation of Itemized Deduction for Cheryl Stafford:	
Adjusted Gross Income	
Medical Expenses Deduction:	
Medical Expenses Paid	
7.5% of gross income	
Medical Expenses Deduction	
Taxes Deduction:	
Real Estate Taxes	
Gifts Deduction:	
Gifts to Charity	
Total Itemized Deduction	

Spreadsheet Directions

1. Start your spreadsheet software program and open problem **SA12.xls.**
2. Record gross income and interest income amounts for Greg Miller to compute his *Total Income.* Deduct Mr. Miller's IRA deduction from that amount.
3. Fill in the amounts for Mr. Miller's standard deduction and exemptions. Subtract standard deduction and exemption amounts from *Adjusted Gross Income* to compute *Taxable Income.*
4. Use the tax rate schedule provided and insert the formula to calculate Mr. Miller's tax due based on his taxable income. Next, adjust his tax due by any tax credits listed.
5. Input the deductions from Mr. Miller's paychecks. If the amount exceeds his tax due, he is entitled to a refund.
6. Repeat the same procedure for Ms. Stafford and Ms. Bowman. For Ms. Stafford, compute her total *Itemized Deduction* amount using the "Computation of Itemized Deduction for Cheryl Stafford" section of your spreadsheet.
7. After you complete the spreadsheet, save your work to a new file labeled **SA12***.xls.** (Replace *** with your initials.)
8. Print out a copy of your work if your teacher has instructed you to do so.

Interpreting Results

1. When completing the final tax returns for each client, which tax form is most appropriate for each client?

   ____

2. What is the taxable income for each of Shelly's clients?

   ____

3. Which of Shelly's clients will receive a tax refund? What is the amount?

   ____

Drawing Conclusions

1. When computing itemized deductions, what types of items should be considered? What criteria are used to determine whether the standard deduction should be used instead? Explain.

   ____
   ____
   ____
   ____
   ____
   ____
   ____
   ____
   ____

Student Class Instructor

Date Assigned Date Completed

2. Explain the difference between an exemption and a standard deduction.

Student Class Instructor

Date Assigned Date Completed

CHAPTER 12 Planning Your Tax Strategy

SELF-ASSESSMENT QUIZ

DIRECTIONS: *Identify the letter of the choice that best completes the statement or answers the question.*

1. The tax a person pays when he or she buys a music CD is (A) sales tax (B) excise tax (C) estate tax (D) gift tax.
2. An example of an inheritance tax is the money collected on (A) a pizza order (B) cigarettes and gasoline (C) a deceased person's money (D) property left in a will.
3. The federal government's leading source of revenue is (A) property taxes (B) sales taxes (C) income taxes (D) Social Security taxes.
4. In which category do tips belong? (A) earned income (B) dividend income (C) interest income (D) tax-deferred income
5. An exemption is subtracted from a person's (A) gross income (B) adjusted gross income (C) taxable income (D) amount of taxes owed.
6. The money a person receives from the government when he or she pays too much in taxes is called a tax (A) liability (B) refund (C) credit (D) exclusion.
7. A W-4 form determines the amount an employee will (A) make in estimated payments (B) pay in taxes (C) receive in Social Security (D) have withheld.
8. If a person cannot file his or her federal tax return by April 15, he or she must file (A) Form 4868 (B) Form 1040EZ (C) a W-2 form (D) Form 1099-INT.
9. Of the following steps, which is the last a person performs when preparing his or her tax return? (A) entering total wages (B) subtracting deductions from adjusted gross income (C) subtracting tax owed from tax withheld (D) claiming an earned income tax credit.
10. Which amounts are tax-deferred? (A) interest paid on mortgage loans (B) real estate taxes (C) interest made on municipal bonds (D) investments in IRAs

Student Class Instructor

Date Assigned Date Completed

CHAPTER 13 Home and Motor Vehicle Insurance

Reviewing Key Terms: Complete the Sentence

DIRECTIONS: *Using terms from the following list, complete the sentences below. Write the letter of the term you have chosen in the space provided.*

A. insurance	D. peril	G. umbrella policy
B. policyholder	E. hazard	H. collision
C. risk	F. household inventory	I. no-fault system
		J. assigned risk pool

1. Defective wiring is an example of a(n) ______ because it increases the likelihood of loss through some peril.
2. The type of insurance that covers damage to the insured's vehicle when it is involved in an accident is ______insurance.
3. A(n) ______ is the purchaser of an insurance policy.
4. A(n) ______ supplements basic personal liability coverage, and is also called a personal catastrophe policy.
5. ______ is protection against possible financial loss.
6. A list or other documentation of personal belongings, with purchase dates and cost information, is a(n) ______.
7. The chance of loss or injury is called ______.
8. Every state has a(n) ______ which includes all the people who cannot get motor vehicle insurance.
9. Each party involved in an accident collects money from his or her own insurance company under a(n) ______.
10. Anything that may possibly cause a loss is a(n) ______.

Student Class Instructor

Date Assigned Date Completed

CHAPTER 13 Home and Motor Vehicle Insurance

Understanding Key Concepts

DIRECTIONS: On a separate sheet of paper, answer the questions below.

1. Classify each of the following items as an insurance peril or insurance hazard: windstorms, earthquakes, icy steps, robbery, faulty brakes, broken locks.
2. Give an example of each kind of risk—personal, property, and liability.
3. Greta is moving into her first apartment and wants to manage the risk of theft. List the four methods of risk management Greta could use and give an example of what each would look like.
4. Pedro is planning to build a home in the San Francisco area. How might he reduce the risk of earthquake damage? How might he shift the risk?
5. List the four questions to ask yourself when planning a risk management plan.
6. Aiko brought her family's laptop to Chile during her semester of study abroad, and it was damaged on the return flight home. Will her parents' homeowners insurance cover the cost of repairs? Explain.
7. Imagine you are Ben's insurance agent. Ben wants to insure his rare violin worth tens of thousands of dollars. What would you recommend?
8. How does medical payments coverage differ from the personal liability portion of a homeowners insurance policy?
9. Walt paid $500 for an old car that he drives to and from work. He wants to save money on vehicle insurance but is required by law to carry insurance that will cover the injuries and property damages of others if he causes an accident. What kinds insurance should Walt buy? What kind does he need least?
10. Name at least five factors that influence the cost of motor vehicle insurance.

Student ______ Class ______ Instructor ______

Date Assigned ______ Date Completed ______

CHAPTER 13 Home and Motor Vehicle Insurance

Activity 1: *Risky Business*

SCANS COMPETENCIES ACHIEVED

Reading, Reasoning, Decision making, Responsibility, Self-management, Acquiring and evaluating information

OBJECTIVE: *Determine which types of insurance might be important for you based on different perils you may encounter.*

Risk assessment and management are important concepts in the world of insurance. Your judgment of how likely it is that you will suffer a particular peril will determine which types of insurance you choose to carry. In this activity, you'll rate a variety of perils along a continuum line, based on how likely you believe they are to affect you.

Read the numbered list of possible perils. Then place the number of the peril at the point along the continuum line that corresponds to how likely you feel the peril is in your life.

1. You will be at fault in a vehicle accident.
2. You will own a home that will need to be protected against natural disasters, theft, and other occurrences.
3. You will become a professional musician and need to insure your hands.
4. Your apartment will be robbed.
5. A tornado will destroy your home and possessions.
6. Someone will trip on your sidewalk and sue you.
7. You will need to rent a vehicle while yours is being repaired after an accident.
8. A child of yours will accidentally break a neighbor's window.
9. Your dog will bite someone.
10. Your vehicle will be hit by an uninsured driver.

Most Likely ●————————————————● **Least Likely**

Now, based on these perils, which three types of insurance would you probably buy?

______

______

______

Student Class Instructor

Date Assigned Date Completed

CHAPTER 13 Home and Motor Vehicle Insurance

Activity 2: *Comparing Two Insurance Quotes*

SCANS COMPETENCIES ACHIEVED

Reading, Writing, Listening, Math, Problem solving, Decision making, Acquiring and evaluating information, Organizing and maintaining information, Participating as a member of a team

OBJECTIVE: *Obtain and compare two different insurance quotes to determine which is the better choice.*

Comparing motor vehicle insurance rates from different insurance companies can save you a considerable amount of money. In this activity, you'll work with a partner to obtain quotes on the same vehicle from two different insurance companies. Then you'll evaluate the quotes, comparing costs, coverages, and other elements to determine which would be the better choice.

First, you and your partner will need to agree on the year, make, and model of the vehicle and the age and gender of the driver. Then you will need to obtain two quotes, either by visiting insurance agents in your area or by getting a quote on the Internet. Use the chart on the next page to make notes about the quotes you receive. Then work together to answer the questions below.

1. Which quote has the higher deductible?

____

2. Which quote seems to offer better coverage? Why?

____

____

____

3. How do liability limits of the two quotes compare?

____

____

____

4. Which insurance would you probably buy? Why?

____

____

____

Student Class Instructor

Date Assigned Date Completed

QUOTE 1

Company Name **Agent Name**

Vehicle Year **Make** **Model** **Driver Age** **M** **F**

Coverages	Limits of Liability	Deductible(s)
Comprehensive Physical Damage		
Collision		
Property Damage Liability		
Bodily Injury Liability		
Medical Payments		
Uninsured Motorist's Protection		
Other Features		

QUOTE 2

Company Name **Agent Name**

Vehicle Year **Make** **Model** **Driver Age** **M** **F**

Coverages	Limits of Liability	Deductible(s)
Comprehensive Physical Damage		
Collision		
Property Damage Liability		
Bodily Injury Liability		
Medical Payments		
Uninsured Motorist's Protection		
Other Features		

Student ____ Class ____ Instructor ____

Date Assigned ____ Date Completed ____

CHAPTER 13 Home and Motor Vehicle Insurance

Math-Building Skills: Does Safety Pay?

Matt and Kristin are newly married and living in their first house. The yearly premium on their homeowners insurance policy is $450 for the coverage they need. Their insurance company offers a 5% discount if they install deadbolt locks on all exterior doors. The couple can also receive a 2% discount if they install smoke detectors on each floor. They have contacted a locksmith, who will provide and install deadbolt locks on the two exterior doors for $60 each. At the local hardware store, smoke detectors cost $8 each, and the new house has two floors. Kristin and Matt can install them themselves.

1. What discount will Matt and Kristin receive if they install the deadbolts? ____

   If they install smoke detectors? ____

2. Assuming their insurance rates remain the same, how many years will it take them to earn back in discounts the cost of the deadbolts? ____

   The cost of the smoke detectors? ____

3. Would you recommend Matt and Kristin invest in the safety items? Why or why not?

____

____

____

____

____

Student ____________________ Class ____________ Instructor ____________

Date Assigned ____________________ Date Completed ____________________

CHAPTER 13 Home and Motor Vehicle Insurance

Your Financial Portfolio Worksheet

Motor Vehicle Insurance—How Much Will It Cost?

Identify a make, model and year of a vehicle you might like to own. Following the worksheet, research two insurance companies and compare prices. You can get their rates by telephone. Many also have Web sites. Record your findings.

Make, model, and year of the vehicle: ____________________

Miles driven per year: ____________________

Miles driven to school and work: ____________________

Vehicle used for driving while on the job? ____________________

	Insurer A	Insurer B
Bodily Injury Coverage: • Bodily injury liability: $50,000 each person; $100,000 each accident • Uninsured motorist's protection • Medical payments coverage: $2,000 each person		
Physical Damage Coverage: • Property damage liability: $50,000 each accident • Collision with $500 deductible • Comprehensive physical damage with $500 deductible		
Car Rental:		
Discounts: good driver, air bags, garage parking		
Annual total		

How do they compare?

____

Which company would you choose and why?

____

____

____

Student Class Instructor

Date Assigned Date Completed

CHAPTER 13 Home and Motor Vehicle Insurance

Finance Online: Choosing a Vehicle with Insurance in Mind

Vehicle insurance premiums take a large bite out of a driver's income. He or she could save money by looking at insurance discounts before buying a vehicle.

Choose two or three new vehicle models. Then use an Internet search engine to find descriptions of standard features on each vehicle. Print out or jot down the information. Next, visit an insurance company's Web site. What discounts does the company offer? Focus on feature-related discounts. Visit as many Web sites as necessary to complete the items below.

Keywords Used	Site Name	Web Site Addresses	Information Offered

1. List your choices of vehicle models and some of their standard features.

2. What feature-related discounts does the insurance company offer?

3. Which of your vehicle choices qualifies for the most discounts? Name the discounts.

Student	Class	Instructor
Date Assigned	Date Completed	

CHAPTER 13 Home and Motor Vehicle Insurance

Software Activity (Optional)

Spreadsheet Application

Evaluating Home and Motor Vehicle Insurance Policy Coverage

OBJECTIVE: *To evaluate home and motor vehicle insurance policies and compute claim coverages.*

Practice Situation

Eric Fowler and his wife Susan just purchased their first home, which cost $130,000. They purchased a homeowners policy to insure the home itself for $120,000 and personal property coverage of $75,000. They declined any coverage for additional living expenses. The deductible for the policy is $500. Eric's Ford Mustang and Susan's Toyota Corolla are insured with the same insurance agent. They have 50/100/15 vehicle insurance coverage.

Soon after Eric and Susan moved into their new home, a strong windstorm caused damage to their roof. They reported the roof damage to be $17,000. While the roof was under repair, the couple had to live in a nearby hotel for three days. The hotel bill amounted to $320. That same week, Susan had an accident. She lost control of her car and hit a parked car and damaged a storefront. The damage to the parked car was $4,300 and the damage to the store was $15,400.

Assuming the insurance company settles claims using the replacement value method, what amount will the insurance company pay for the damages to the roof? What amount will the insurance company pay for Susan's car accident? Use the following spreadsheet to make your computations.

Home Damages	
Home value	
Insured Amount	
Damage amount reported	
Additional living expenses incurred	
Total expenses incurred from wind storm	
Deductible on the policy	
Insurance company covered amount	
Eric and Susan's costs	
Car Accident	
Store damage amount	
Parked car damage amount	
Total damages	
Insurance company covered amount	
Eric and Susan's costs	

Spreadsheet Directions

1. Start your spreadsheet software program and open problem SA13.xls.
2. Record the value of Eric and Susan's home along with the insured amounts for the structure and personal property. Format all dollar amounts to Currency, decimal places 0.
3. Next, record the amount of roof damage reported and the cost of additional living expenses incurred.
4. Using the information presented about Eric and Susan's homeowners policy, compute the amount of damage that will be covered by the insurance company. Calculate the total amount that Susan and Eric will have to pay for this occurrence.
5. Now, review the information about Susan's car accident. Record the damage amounts for the parked car and storefront. Insert the formula to compute the total damages.
6. Record the amount that will be covered by the insurance company for property damages. Then insert the formula to calculate the remaining amount that Susan and Eric will have to pay for the accident.
7. Complete the spreadsheet, then save your work to a new file labeled **SA13***.xls.** (Replace *** with your initials.)
8. Print out a copy of your work if your teacher has instructed you to do so.

Interpreting Results

1. What amount will the insurance company pay for the damage to Eric and Susan's roof? ____________________
2. What amount will Susan and Eric have to pay for Susan's car accident? ____________________
3. What amount will the insurance company pay for Susan's car accident? ____________________
4. Based on the information presented, what bodily injury coverage is included in Eric and Susan's motor vehicle insurance policy?

____

Drawing Conclusions

1. If Eric and Susan's vehicle coverage had been 50/100/25, what impact would this have had on the amount they owed for this accident? Explain.

____

____

____

2. If items inside Eric and Susan's home had been damaged as a result of the windstorm, would these items have been covered by their homeowners policy? Explain.

____

____

____

Student Class Instructor

Date Assigned Date Completed

CHAPTER 13 Home and Motor Vehicle Insurance

SELF-ASSESSMENT QUIZ

DIRECTIONS: *Identify the letter of the choice that best completes the statement or answers the question.*

1. Which insurance term refers to anything that may cause a loss? (A) risk (B) peril (C) hazard (D) liability
2. A risk that is NOT insurable is known as a (A) pure risk (B) personal risk (C) liability risk (D) speculative risk.
3. Refusing to smoke for health purposes is an example of the risk management method known as risk (A) reduction (B) avoidance (C) assumption (D) shifting.
4. An insurance policy with a deductible is a combination of (A) risk avoidance and risk reduction (B) risk assumption and risk reduction (C) risk shifting and risk assumption (D) risk reduction and risk shifting.
5. The personal liability portion of a homeowners insurance policy protects the insured against financial loss when his or her (A) house floods (B) jewelry is stolen (C) guests injure themselves (D) reputation is damaged.
6. Renters insurance includes coverage for all the following items EXCEPT (A) the building (B) personal property (C) additional living expenses (D) personal liability.
7. The basic home insurance policy form protects against several perils, including (A) sleet (B) lightning (C) flood (D) earthquake.
8. Home insurance rates are lower for houses (A) built of wood (B) near fire hydrants (C) in a high-crime area (D) costing $300,000 or more.
9. What kind of motor vehicle insurance provides protection to the policyholder if he or she is injured by a hit-and-run driver? (A) property damage liability (B) uninsured motorist's protection (C) collision insurance (D) comprehensive physical damage coverage
10. An assigned risk pool includes the people in a state who (A) are under 25 (B) drive the same make car (C) live in big cities (D) cannot get coverage.

Student _______ Class _______ Instructor _______

Date Assigned _______ Date Completed _______

CHAPTER 14 Health, Disability, and Life Insurance

Reviewing Key Terms: Complete the Sentence

DIRECTIONS: *Using terms from the following list, complete the sentences below. Write the letter of the item you have chosen in the space provided.*

A. beneficiary	E. preferred provider organization (PPO)	H. term insurance
B. stop-loss	F. Medicare	I. cash value
C. Medicaid	G. disability income insurance	J. rider
D. managed care		

1. Certain low-income individuals and families can qualify for a government medical assistance program called ______.
2. A federally funded health insurance program available mainly to people over 65 and people with certain disabilities is ______.
3. A ______ changes the terms of an insurance policy by adding or excluding conditions or by altering benefits.
4. Whole life insurance can serve as an investment because it has a ______.
5. Medical policies with a ______ provision require an insurance policyholder to pay all costs up to a certain amount, after which insurance pays 100 percent of covered expenses.
6. Prepaid health plans that provide comprehensive health care to their members are called ______ plans.
7. A group of doctors and hospitals that agree to provide specified medical services to members at prearranged fees is called a ______.
8. ______ provides protection against loss of life for only a specified period of time.
9. ______ is available to provide regular cash income if you are unable to work due to nonwork-related injuries or illness.
10. A ______ is the person named to receive the benefits from an insurance policy.

Student Class Instructor

Date Assigned Date Completed

CHAPTER 14 Health, Disability, and Life Insurance

Understanding Key Concepts

DIRECTIONS: *On a separate sheet of paper, answer the questions below.*

1. How does medical expense insurance differ from disability income insurance?
2. Andrew's employer offers a group insurance plan that covers hospital stays and surgical procedures. The company that employs his wife Shirley offers an insurance plan that covers these things as well as doctor visits and prescriptions. Shirley finds out that her insurance has a COB provision. How does this help Andrew?
3. Why might a person choose to buy individual health insurance?
4. Raj is thinking about buying major medical insurance to supplement his basic health insurance from work. Describe a situation in which Raj would need major medical.
5. How do HMOs help prevent future medical problems?
6. Olga's health plan uses a network of physicians who have contracted to provide services for certain fees. A plan physician manages her care and refers her to specialists. However, Olga uses a dermatologist outside the network even though the plan charges her more. What kind of plan does Olga have—an HMO, a PPO, or a POS?
7. Mr. Carstens, a physical education instructor, broke his hip while demonstrating wrestling holds to his students. He will not be able to teach for at least a semester. The school district's insurance plan does not offer disability benefits. For what other kinds of disability income might he be eligible?
8. Josefa is trying to decide which disability income insurance to buy. One policy will pay 75 percent of her take-home pay for life if she becomes permanently disabled. The other policy will pay 75 percent of her take home pay until she is 65 but has a much lower premium than the first. Which policy would you recommend? Why?
9. Why is term life insurance often the best value for customers?
10. What is credit life insurance used for?

Student   Class   Instructor

Date Assigned   Date Completed

CHAPTER 14 Health, Disability, and Life Insurance

Activity 1: *Analyzing Types of Insurance*

SCANS COMPETENCIES ACHIEVED

Writing, Reading, Creative thinking, Responsibility, Self-management, Acquiring and evaluating information, Interpreting and communicating information

OBJECTIVE: *Review concepts about health, disability, and life insurance and apply these concepts to students' own lives.*

On this page are three columns, one each for health insurance, disability insurance, and life insurance. Fill in the solid lines with descriptive details from the chapter about each kind of insurance. On the dotted lines, write phrases that describe how each type of insurance can affect your own life. A partial sample answer is provided.

health insurance	life insurance	disability insurance
helps ease financial burden of		
expensive health care		
could prevent major debt if I		
get into an accident		

Student ____________________ Class ____________ Instructor ____________

Date Assigned ____________________ Date Completed ____________________

CHAPTER 14 Health, Disability, and Life Insurance

Activity 2: *Comparing Health Insurance Plans*

SCANS COMPETENCIES ACHIEVED

Reading, Writing, Listening, Speaking, Acquiring and evaluating information, Organizing and maintaining information

OBJECTIVE: *Compare health insurance plans.*

This chapter emphasized the importance of comparing health insurance plans from different sources. In this activity, you'll obtain and evaluate information on three different types of health insurance policies.

On the next page, you'll find a chart that has columns for three different health insurance providers. You'll need to choose one health maintenance organization (HMO) that does business in your area. Your second provider should be a private insurance company; you can find companies in the telephone book under "Insurance." Find out about the individual policies that the company offers. Your third provider should be a local business that offers a plan to its employees. Contact the Human Relations department at that business to get information about its group policies for employees.

For each provider, find out which kinds of insurance it offers, what its premiums are, and how much the deductibles and coinsurance are. Then, on the lines below, write a paragraph explaining which policy would be the best for you and why.

Provider	(HMO)	(private policy)	(group policy)
Premium			
Hospital Expense Insurance			
Surgical Expense Insurance			
Physician Expense Insurance			
Major Medical Insurance			
Comprehensive Major Medical Insurance			
Other benefits (dental, vision, long-term care, etc.)			

Student Class Instructor

Date Assigned Date Completed

CHAPTER 14 Health, Disability, and Life Insurance

Math-Building Skills: Stop-loss vs. Coinsurance

DIRECTIONS: *Sarah's comprehensive major medical health insurance plan at work has a deductible of $750. The policy pays 85% of any amount above the deductible. While on a hiking trip, she contracted a rare bacterial disease. Her medical costs for treatment, including medicines, tests, and a six-day hospital stay totaled $8,893. A friend told her that she would have paid less if she had a policy with a stop-loss feature that capped her out-of-pocket expenses at $3,000. Was her friend correct? Show your computations in the space below. Then, on the lines, write which policy would have cost Sarah less and by how much.*

Student ______ Class ______ Instructor ______

Date Assigned ______ Date Completed ______

CHAPTER 14 Health, Disability, and Life Insurance

Your Financial Portfolio Worksheet

Buying Life Insurance

To compare life insurance rates, use the Internet or visit, telephone, or write two different insurance companies to obtain information.

Base the quote on (1) a 20-year decreasing term insurance policy for $100,000 and (b) a whole life insurance policy for $100,000. Use your own age.

Type of Policy	Company A	Company B
20-year decreasing term insurance $100,000		
Monthly premium		
Total premiums, 20 years		
Cash value at 20 years	none	none
Whole life insurance (limited payment) $100,000		
Monthly premium		
Total premiums, 20 years		
Cash value at 20 years		

1. Which is less expensive, term insurance or whole life insurance?

   ______ term ______ whole life

2. Which company would you select for your purchase of life insurance? Why?

   ______

   ______

Student _______________ Class _______________ Instructor _______________

Date Assigned _______________ Date Completed _______________

CHAPTER 14 Health, Disability, and Life Insurance

Finance Online: Exploring Insurance

Choose a type of insurance to research on the Internet—health, life, or disability. What information would you need to purchase one of these types of insurance? Visit Web sites that offer information about purchasing insurance. Use the information to answer the questions below.

Keywords Used	Site Names	Web Site Addresses	Information Offered

1. How do factors such as age, physical condition, and salary affect the premium you might have to pay for insurance coverage? Give two examples.

____

____

____

2. Besides Web sites of companies that sell insurance, what sites provide helpful information to consumers who are in the market for insurance? List two.

____

____

3. List three questions you would ask an insurance agent who was trying to sell you this type of insurance plan.

____

____

Student Class Instructor

Date Assigned Date Completed

CHAPTER 14 Health, Disability, and Life Insurance

Software Activity (Optional)

Spreadsheet Application

Comparing POS, HMO, and Private Insurance Coverages

OBJECTIVE: *To evaluate and compare the costs associated with three major forms of health insurance.*

Practice Situation

Ronald Roth started his new job as Controller with Aerosystems today. Carole, the employee benefits clerk, has given Ronald a packet that contains information on the company's health insurance options. Aerosystems offers its employees the choice between a private insurance company plan, an HMO, and a POS. Ronald needs to review the packet and make a decision on which health care program fits his needs. The following is an overview of that information.

1) Private insurance company plan: The monthly premium cost to Ronald will be $42.32. For all doctor office visits, prescriptions, and major medical charges, Ronald will be responsible for 20% and the insurance company will cover 80% of covered charges. The annual deductible is $500.
2) The HMO is provided to employees free of charge. The copayment for doctor's office visits and major medical charges is $10. Prescription copayments are $5. The HMO pays 100% after Ronald's copayment. The HMO does not have an annual deductible.
3) The POS requires that the employee pay $24.44 per month to supplement cost of the program with the company's payment. If Ron uses health care providers within the network plan, he pays the copayments as described above for the HMO. He can also choose to use a health care provider out of the service and pay 20% of all charges, after he pays a $500 deductible. The POS will pay for 80% of those covered visits. The POS does not have an annual deductible.

Ronald has decided to review his medical bills from the previous year to see what costs he incurred and to help him evaluate his choices. He visited his general physician four times during the year at a cost of $125 for each visit. He also spent $65 and $89 on prescriptions during the year. Using these costs as an example, what would Ron pay for each of the plans described above? (For the purposes of the POS computation, assume that Ron visited a physician outside of the network plan. Assume he had his prescriptions filled at a network-approved pharmacy.)

Student ____________________ Class ____________________ Instructor ____________________

Date Assigned ____________________ Date Completed ____________________

	Private Insurance Ron's Annual Costs	HMO Ron's Annual Costs	POS Ron's Annual Costs
Ronald's annual premium costs			
Sample medical costs:			
4 office visits			
2 prescriptions			
Total Medical Costs			

Spreadsheet Directions

1. Start your spreadsheet software program and open problem **SA14.xls.**
2. Insert the formula to compute the annual premium charges for each insurance option.
3. Using Ronald's sample medical expenses, insert formulas to compute his charges for four office visits and two prescription charges for each plan. Remember to consider the $500 deductible that Ron is responsible for under the private insurance company plan and the POS plan.
4. Insert the formulas to total annual medical charges.
5. Format all dollar amounts to Currency, decimal places 2.
6. Perform your calculations and complete the spreadsheet, then save your work to a new file labeled **SA14***.xls.** (Replace *** with your initials.)
7. Print out a copy of your work if your teacher has instructed you to do so.

Interpreting Results

1. What annual medical costs will Ronald pay using the sample medical expenses provided if he were to enroll in the private insurance company plan?

____

____

2. What total medical costs will Ronald pay if he enrolls in the HMO plan?

____

Student Class Instructor

Date Assigned Date Completed

3. If Ronald selects the POS plan, what annual medical costs did you compute?

Drawing Conclusions

1. Discuss the benefits you see of the POS plan that Ronald has been offered.

2. In addition to the financial considerations in choosing a health care plan, list other concerns that Ronald should evaluate when making this decision. Explain.

Student Class Instructor

Date Assigned Date Completed

CHAPTER 14 Health, Disability, and Life Insurance

SELF-ASSESSMENT QUIZ

DIRECTIONS: *Identify the letter of the choice that best completes the statement or answers the question.*

1. Medical expense insurance covers all the following costs of being ill EXCEPT (A) hospital stays (B) lost income (C) doctors' visits (D) medications.
2. Under basic health insurance, anesthesia is considered a (A) hospital expense (B) surgical expense (C) physician expense (D) major medical expense.
3. A policy with aggregate limits will limit only the (A) daily cost of a hospital stay (B) total amount of coverage (C) policyholder's out-of-pocket expenses (D) percentage of coinsurance.
4. Which is the statewide organization that provides hospital care benefits? (A) Blue Cross (B) Blue Shield (C) Medicare (D) Medicaid
5. One advantage of a preferred provider organization (PPO) over a health maintenance organization (HMO) is that the PPO covers (A) preventive services (B) emergency care (C) visits to any doctor (D) home health care.
6. Medicare's hospital insurance covers (A) hospice care (B) long-term nursing care (C) routine checkups (D) most immunizations.
7. Worker's compensation pays benefits to people when they (A) pay Social Security (B) are covered by an HMO (C) lose income because of illness (D) are injured on the job.
8. The ideal disability income insurance provides (A) payments that continue for life (B) 40 percent of the policyholder's income (C) coverage after accidents only (D) benefits after a long elimination period.
9. Which type of life insurance lets a policyholder change from term to permanent coverage? (A) decreasing term (B) multiyear level term (C) renewable term (D) conversion term
10. Beneficiaries wait two years before receiving full death benefits under a common policy feature called (A) the incontestability clause (B) a waiver of premium disability (C) the suicide clause (D) double indemnity.

Student ______ Class ______ Instructor ______

Date Assigned ______ Date Completed ______

CHAPTER 15 Retirement and Estate Planning

Reviewing Key Terms: Complete the Sentence

DIRECTIONS: *Using terms from the following list, complete the sentences below. Write the letter of the item you have chosen in the space provided.*

A. assisted-living facility	D. vesting	G. estate
B. defined-contribution plan	E. individual retirement account (IRA)	H. beneficiaries
C. 401(k) plan	F. Keogh plan	I. intestate
		J. probate

1. A(n) ______ sets up an individual pension account for each employee and specifies the amount the employer will contribute annually.
2. The point at which an employee becomes eligible to receive a company's contributions to his or her pension plan is ______.
3. A retirement plan especially designed for self-employed people and their employees is a(n) ______.
4. A residence complex that provides personal and medical services for the elderly is a(n) ______.
5. A person's ______ consists of everything he or she owns.
6. People named to receive a portion of the estate after the estate's owner dies are called ______.
7. A retirement savings plan created especially for one person is known as a(n) ______.
8. ______ refers to a person who does not have a valid will.
9. The legal procedure of proving a will to be valid or invalid is ______.
10. ______ is a retirement plan in which employees set aside a portion of their salary from each paycheck to be deducted from their gross pay and placed in a special account.

Student Class Instructor

Date Assigned Date Completed

CHAPTER 15 Retirement and Estate Planning

Understanding Key Concepts

DIRECTIONS: *On a separate sheet of paper, answer the questions below.*

1. Many people believe that saving just a little toward retirement does not help. Make an argument against this.
2. How can a person's housing choice help him or her reach retirement goals?
3. Why should a person take inflation into account when estimating retirement expenses?
4. Moira's grandmother is in good health but longs to quit her job and travel. She is thinking about retiring at 63 and relying on her Social Security benefits to pay living expenses. Moira is trying to persuade her grandmother to continue working until she is 67. What reasons might Moira give?
5. Harold paid taxes on his annual contributions to his retirement account and started withdrawing money when he turned 61 years old. The withdrawals are tax- and penalty-free. What type of retirement account does Harold have?
6. Samantha is retired. She receives all the payments to which she is entitled and takes advantage of low-cost recreation opportunities such as the park and the library. She also uses her senior discount on movie tickets, meals, and entrance fees for state and national parks. However, she finds the cost of retirement higher than she anticipated. What should she do?
7. How do a traditional marital share will and an exemption trust will differ?
8. What are three advantages a living trust has compared with a will?
9. List three major types of taxes imposed on estates.
10. Eleanor is concerned that the taxes, probate costs, and other expenses surrounding her death will create a burden for her daughters. How can she provide them with tax-free cash to help settle her estate?

Student	Class	Instructor
Date Assigned	Date Completed	

CHAPTER 15 Retirement and Estate Planning

Activity 1: *Getting Ready to Write a Will*

> **SCANS COMPETENCIES ACHIEVED**
> Reading, Writing, Problem solving, Decision making, Reasoning, Seeing things in the mind's eye, Responsibility

OBJECTIVE: *Think through your assets and possessions in preparation for writing a will.*

Thinking about your own death is an unpleasant task, but something that might be *even more* distressing is what would happen if you died without a will and had no say in how your assets were divided. Dying without a will leaves your assets in the hands of a probate court, which will divide them up as it sees fit, not as you may have wanted. In this activity, you'll make an inventory of your assets, financial and otherwise, and explore what you'd like to happen to them in case of your untimely death.

In the first column at the bottom of this page, list items you'd like to include in your will. Include all financial assets, like cash, savings, stocks, bonds, mutual funds, and other investments you imagine having. Then think about items that may have cost a good deal: a car or bike, computer, stereo system, musical instrument, or sports and hobby equipment. Finally, consider inexpensive items that may have sentimental or other special value to a friend or relative, such as a piece of jewelry, an old letter or photograph, or a favorite memento. In the second column, write to whom you'd like to give the item. In the third column, explain why you've decided to give that item to that particular person. Use extra paper if you need more space.

Financial Assets	To Whom?	Why?
Major Possessions		
Items of Sentimental or Special Value		

Student Class Instructor

Date Assigned Date Completed

CHAPTER 15 Retirement and Estate Planning

Activity 2: *Researching the Retirement Plans of Area Businesses*

SCANS COMPETENCIES ACHIEVED

Reading, Writing, Listening, Acquiring and evaluating information, Organizing and maintaining information, Interpreting and communicating information

OBJECTIVE: *Research and evaluate the retirement programs of a local business.*

These days, when people decide where they might like to work, they usually consider more than just the salary. The benefits package a company offers is playing a bigger and bigger role in people's employment decisions. One of the most important job benefits a company can offer is the retirement program. Successful companies know that one way to attract the most talented workers is to offer a generous and flexible retirement program. In this activity, you'll research and evaluate the retirement plans offered by some area businesses.

Working with a partner, begin by brainstorming a short list of some of the best-known and most successful companies in your community. Then look over the chart on the next page. Each of you will choose one company and contact its human resources or personnel office. Arrange to obtain a brochure about the company's retirement program or interview a human resources employee. Record the information on the chart. After you have both obtained information about one company, get together and compare the two retirement plans. Then, write a paragraph explaining which company you feel has the better retirement program and why.

	Your company	Your partner's company
Name of company		
Source of information		
Program(s) available		
401(k) description		
Does company match 401(k) contributions?		
What are the employee investment options?		
Other information		

Which company has the better retirement program? Why?

____

____

____

____

____

____

Student ______ Class ______ Instructor ______

Date Assigned ______ Date Completed ______

CHAPTER 15 Retirement and Estate Planning

Math-Building Skills: Retirement Planning

One key element of retirement planning is estimating how much money you'll need in retirement and determining how much to save now to make sure you reach your goals.

Janine Randolph is 25 and has a good job at a biotechnology company. She currently has $5,000 in an IRA, an important part of her retirement nest egg. She believes her IRA will grow at an annual rate of 8%, and she plans to leave it untouched until she retires at age 65. Janine estimates that she will need $875,000 in her *total* retirement nest egg by the time she is 65 in order to have a retirement income of $20,000 a year (she expects that Social Security will pay her an additional $15,000 a year).

1. How much will Janine's IRA be worth when she needs to start withdrawing money from it when she retires? [There is a special formula for determining how much this sum of money will grow. Multiply the original amount by **21.724** to find how much it will become after 40 years.]

   ______

2. How much money will she have to accumulate in her company's 401(k) plan over the next 40 years in order to reach her retirement income goal?

   ______

Student | Class | Instructor

Date Assigned | Date Completed

CHAPTER 15 Retirement and Estate Planning

Your Financial Portfolio Worksheet

Saving for Retirement

Calculate how much you would have in 10 years if you saved $2,000 a year at an annual interest rate of 10 percent, with the company contributing $500 a year.

	Contributions	10% Interest	Total
Annual contribution of 10% of a $20,000 salary	$2,000.00		
Company annual contribution matching of 2.5% of the salary	500.00		
1st Year			
2nd Year			
3rd Year			
4th Year			
5th Year			
6th Year			
7th Year			
8th Year			
9th Year			
10th Year			
Total			

Student | Class | Instructor

Date Assigned | Date Completed

CHAPTER 15 Retirement and Estate Planning

Finance Online: Planning to Give

Charitable gifts can be an important tool in estate planning. Giving to charity supports a cause and offers benefits such as reduced taxes and increased interest income.

To find ways to plan an estate and help your favorite charities at the same time, use the Internet to find at least three Web sites that suggest general ways to combine estate planning and charitable giving. At the Web sites, look for specific details about planned giving.

Keywords Used	Site Name	Web Site Addresses	Information Offered

1. What basic approaches to estate planning through charitable giving did you find?

2. Which Web sites suggest using donations in estate planning?

3. Choose a charity that accepts donations from people's wills. How does the charity use these gifts?

Student Class Instructor

Date Assigned Date Completed

CHAPTER 15 Retirement and Estate Planning

Software Activity (Optional)

Quicken Application

Reviewing Performance of Retirement Investments

OBJECTIVE: *To utilize Quicken graphing and reporting tools to evaluate the performance of a retirement investment.*

Practice Situation

Stephanie Brown started her retirement account a few years ago. Her employer offers a 401(k) investment plan. She contributed $5,000 on January 1, 2006, and invested in a growth fund, considered to be a higher risk investment. She is attracted by the potential for large returns. The fund focuses on large-cap funds in the energy, utility, and financial services sectors. When she reviewed the prospectus for this fund, she noted that the historical 5-year return was 26.5%. Stephanie recorded her initial investment using Quicken.

Dividends are paid quarterly and are reinvested in the fund. Stephanie contributed another $620 into her 401(k) in April of 2007. From January 2006 to April 2008, Stephanie recorded all dividend payments in Quicken.

Stephanie would like to review the performance of her investment. She would also like to know how much she has earned in dividends since she has participated in the fund. Use Quicken graphing and reporting tools to create and print the following items:

- Investment Performance Graph
- Investment Income Report

Student _______ Class _______ Instructor _______

Date Assigned _______ Date Completed _______

Quicken Directions

1. Start your Quicken software program and open the file **SA15.gdf.**
2. Click **Reports** in the top menu, then select *Investing.*
3. Choose the *Investment Income* report. Input the **From** date as 1/1/06 and the **To** date as 3/1/08. Subtotal by *Year.*
4. Circle **Print** in the top of the Investment Income window.
5. Once the report has printed, click **Reports** again from the top menu selections. Then click *Investing.*
6. Choose the *Investment Performance* report. Input the **From** date as 1/1/06 and the **To** date as 3/1/08. Click the *Graph* tab.
7. Change the **Subtotal By** field to *Security*. This graph depicts the performance and the annual return on the market value of the security.
8. To print this graph, click **Print** in the top of the Investment Income window.
9. Change the **Subtotal By** field to *Account*. This graph depicts the performance and the total return of the investment account.
10. Print this graph by clicking the **Print** button.
11. Once your reports have printed, close your Quicken program and answer the questions that follow.

Interpreting Results

1. Based on the Average Annual Total Return by Security graph for 1/1/06–3/1/08, what is the approximate portfolio value at March 2008? _______________
2. Click the Account button just above the graphs. Based on the Average Annual Total Return by Account for 1/1/06–3/1/08, what is the approximate percentage return on the account? _______________
3. Based on the Investment Income Report by Year for 1/1/06 through 3/1/08, what Dividend Income was reported for 1/06–12/06? What Dividend Income was reported for the overall period? _______________

Drawing Conclusions

1. Is Stephanie's 401(k) investment overperforming or underperforming based on the 5-year historical performance from the investment's prospectus? Explain.

____

____

____

2. When consumers compare retirement investment opportunities, what factors should they consider? Explain.

Student Class Instructor

Date Assigned Date Completed

CHAPTER 15 Retirement and Estate Planning

SELF-ASSESSMENT QUIZ

DIRECTIONS: *Identify the letter of the choice that best completes the statement or answers the question.*

1. A person can save $1 million for retirement if he or she puts $127 per month in investment funds at 11 percent interest starting at age (A) 25 (B) 40 (C) 50 (D) 65.
2. A person in retirement usually spends less than before on (A) recreation (B) transportation (C) medical care (D) health insurance.
3. At what age does a worker generally qualify for reduced benefits from Social Security? (A) 59½ (B) 62 (C) 65 (D) 67
4. An example of a defined-contribution plan is a (A) Veterans Administration pension (B) Roth IRA (C) profit sharing plan (D) Keogh plan.
5. By age 70½, a person must start withdrawing from his or her tax-deferred retirement plan, unless it is a(n) (A) educational IRA (B) Keogh plan (C) 403(b) plan (D) Roth IRA.
6. The spouse eventually receives all the assets of the deceased with a (A) simple will (B) traditional marital share will (C) living will (D) stated dollar amount will.
7. The role of an executor includes all the following tasks EXCEPT (A) choosing a guardian (B) filing income tax returns (C) collecting money due (D) paying debts.
8. The spouse of a deceased person can avoid paying federal taxes on a certain amount of the assets left to him or her under the terms of a (A) testamentary trust (B) living trust (C) credit-shelter trust (D) revocable trust.
9. Only state governments impose (A) income taxes on trusts (B) estate taxes (C) inheritance taxes (D) gift taxes.
10. The best way to handle taxes related to settling an estate is to (A) set aside cash ahead of time (B) buy a life insurance policy (C) have survivors sell assets (D) have survivors make installment payments.

Notes

Notes

Notes

Notes

Notes

Notes

Notes